The Verbal Piece in Ebira

Summer Institute of Linguistics and
The University of Texas at Arlington
Publications in Linguistics

Publication 85

Editors

Virgil Poulter
University of Texas
at Arlington

William R. Merrifield
Summer Institute of
Linguistics

Assistant Editors

Alan C. Wares

Iris M. Wares

Consulting Editors

Doris A. Bartholomew
Pamela M. Bendor-Samuel
Desmond C. Derbyshire
Robert A. Dooley
Jerold A. Edmondson

Austin Hale
Robert E. Longacre
Eugene E. Loos
Kenneth L. Pike
Viola G. Waterhouse

The Verbal Piece in Ebira

by

John R. Adive

A Publication of
The Summer Institute of Linguistics
and
The University of Texas at Arlington
1989

© 1989 by the Summer Institute of Linguistics, Inc.
Library of Congress Catalog No: 88-062276
ISBN: 0-88312-037-2
ISSN: 1040-0850

All Rights Reserved

No part of this publication may be reproduced, stored in a retrieval system, or transmitted in any form or by any means—electronic, mechanical, photocopy, recording, or otherwise—without the express permission of the Summer Institute of Linguistics, with the exception of brief excerpts in journal articles or reviews.

Reprint 1990

Copies of this and other publications of the Summer Institute of Linguistics may be obtained from

    International Academic Bookstore
    Summer Institute of Linguistics
    7500 W. Camp Wisdom Rd.
    Dallas, TX 75236

Contents

Acknowledgments ix
Abbreviations xi
Symbols xii

1 Introduction 1
  1.1 The Ebira People and the Ebira Language 1
  1.2 The Language Name 2
  1.3 Neighboring Languages 2
      Map 1. Nigeria 3
      Map 2. Kwara state 4
      Map 3. Ebira area 5
  1.4 Language Family Affiliation 6
  1.5 Literature Survey 7
  1.6 The Present Study 8
  1.7 The Theoretical Basis of the Study 9

2 Phonology 11
  2.1 The Syllable Structure 11
  2.2 The Vowel Phonemes 16
  2.3 Vowel Harmony 23
  2.4 Syllabic Nasals 34

2.5 The Consonant Phonemes 35
2.6 Tone 40

3 Syntactic Junctures 45
   3.1 Vowel Elision 45
   3.2 Labial Syllable Prosody 55
   3.3 Palatal Syllable Prosody 57
   3.4 Tone Changes 61
   3.5 High Tone as a Syntactic Juncture Feature 65

4 The Verbal Piece: Phrase Rank 69
   4.1 The Verbal Piece 69
   4.2 The Grammatical Hierarchy 69
   4.3 The Verbal Phrase 71
   4.4 Tense 76
      Figure 1. Tense (Indicative Mood)—Harmony Set A 78
      Figure 1. Tense (Indicative Mood)—Harmony Set B 79
   4.5 Mood 83
      Figure 2. Mood—Harmony Set A 84
      Figure 2. Mood—Harmony Set B 85
   4.6 Negative Polarity 90
      Figure 3. Negative Polarity—Harmony Set A 92
      Figure 3. Negative Polarity—Harmony Set B 93
   4.7 Dependent Clauses 96
      Figure 4. Dependent Clauses—Harmony Set A 98
      Figure 4. Dependent Clauses—Harmony Set B 99
   4.8 Pluralization 101

5 The Verbal Piece: Clause Rank 107
   5.1 The Clause 107
   5.2 Transitive Clause 108

5.3 Ditransitive Clause 109

5.4 Semitransitive Clause .111

5.5 Intransitive Clause 113

5.6 Stative Clause 113

5.7 Equative Clause 115

5.8 Copula Clause 116

5.9 The Pronoun System in the Clause 117

5.10 Interrogation and Interrogative Words in the Clause 122

6 The Verbal Piece: Serial Verb Constructions 127

6.1 The Serial Verb Construction 127

6.2 Syntactic Characteristics of Serial Verb Constructions 127
    in Kwa Languages

6.3 The Verbal Status of Serial Verbs 128

6.4 Types of Serial Verb Constructions in Ebira 129

6.5 Auxiliary Verbs 138

7 Analyzed Text 139

Appendices 147

A. A Chart of Monosyllabic Verbs 147

B. A List of Monosyllabic Verbs 151

C. Sample Spectrograms .155

Bibliography 161

Acknowledgments

This revised manuscript is the result of a work which was originally submitted in 1984 for the degree of Doctor of Philosophy in the Department of Phonetics and Linguistics of the University of London. I am extremely grateful to my Supervisor, Professor J. Carnochan for his patient and perceptive help in the writing of this work. I have learned much through Professor Carnochan's careful guidance and practical approach to specific language problems.

I would also like to thank the Nigeria Bible Translation Trust for sponsoring me for this study. I refer especially to Mr. Barnaba Dusu and other members of the Executive Committee of the Trust. The Federal Government of Nigeria Scholarship Board awarded me a scholarship for the last two years of this study for which I am sincerely grateful. My thanks are also due to the Committee of Vice-Chancellors and Principals fo the Universities of the United Kingdom for their award of part of my fees for two sessions under the Overseas Research Students Fees Support Scheme.

Some technical help came from Mr. John Picton of the Africa Department of the School of Oriental and African Studies of the University of London, who shared with me many of his Ebira tape recordings and materials on Ebira anthropology. I am grateful to him. Drs. John Bendor-Samuel and Ron Stanford of the Summer Institute of Linguistics have given much help and encouragement throughout. Dr. Katharine Barnwell spent many hours reading the manuscript and helping me check technical details and accuracy. I am grateful for all the help rendered.

Thanks to Miss Jo Kent for typing the final manuscript of my thesis. I also wish to express my appreciation to each person in the Academic Publications Department of the Summer Institute of Linguistics who has assisted in further editing and formatting of this work so that it may now appear in published form.

I owe tremendous gratitude to many friends in Nigeria, the United Kingdom, and the United States of America who supported me and my family during the period of this study program.

I am deeply grateful to my dear wife, Martha, and my children, Gloria, John (Jr.), Ruth, and James for their patience, understanding and support over a long period.

Abbreviations

1s	first person singular	NP_o	Object Noun Phrase
2s	second person singular	NP_s	Subject Noun Phrase
2pl	second person plural	NUM	Number
3s	third person singular	P	Particle
AdvP	Adverbial Phrase	pl	plural
C	consonant	PN	Pronoun
Cl	Clause	Pr	Pronoun
cont	continuous	pres	present
cop	copula	prev	preverb
Dep	Dependent	quest	question
eq	equative	S	sentence
H	High tone	s	syllable
H'	Down Step (tone)	semitrans	semitransitive
HF	High-Falling tone	sg	singular
Ind	Independent	st	stative
inter	interrogative	subj	subject
intr	intransitive	SVC	Serial Verb Construction
L	Low tone	T	tone
LGA	local government area	TP	Time Particle
LR	Low-Rising tone	trans	transitive
M	Mid tone	V	vowel
N	Noun	Vb	Verb
n	nucleus (of syllable)	vd	voiced
narr	narrative (particle)	vls	voiceless
NP	Noun Phrase	VP	Verb Phrase

Symbols

Except where indicated all examples are written phonemically in Ebira practical orthography. The phonetic manifestations of phoneme units are described in §2.2 and §2.5.

Symbols are used as in the International Phonetic Alphabet (IPA) with the following exceptions adapted for practical purposes:

Adapted Symbols	I P A
i̩	ɪ
u̩	ω
e̩	ɛ
o̩	ɔ
c	tʃ
j	dʒ
y	j

Tone symbols are discussed in 2.6.

1 Introduction

1.1 The Ebira People and the Ebira Language

The Ebira language is spoken by approximately 1,000,000 people.[1] The entire Ebira territory lies southwest of the confluence of the Niger and the Benue, the two main rivers of Nigeria (see Map 1), and comprises what used to be called the Igbirra Division of Kabba Province. The main dialect of Ebira is spoken in the same land area which is now referred to as the six local government areas (LGAs)[2] of Adavi, Okehi, Ageva, Ihima, Okene, and Ajaokuta out of the fourteen LGAs of Kwara State. The six LGAs are shaded in the map of Kwara State (Map 2). Other dialects of Ebira are spoken locally in the following towns, whose names are written in the map of Ebira Territory (Map 3).

(a) Koton-Karfe, a town in Kogi LGA of Kwara State,
(b) Toto and Umaisha, two towns in Nassarawa LGA of Plateau State,
(c) Igara, a town in Auchi LGA of Bendel State.

These towns are, in fact, linguistic islands where Ebira is spoken, surrounded by other languages in their immediate neighborhoods.

This study is of my mother tongue, the main dialect. I come from the town of Ovehira in Ageva LGA, one of the major towns shown in the map of Ebira land (Map 3).

---

[1]The 1963 census lists a population of 500,000 for the then Igbirra Division of Kabba Province. There has not been any accurate national census since then. But the population has since doubled. The estimate normally quoted in current publications for Ebira people is between 800,500 and 1,000,000.

[2]There were six LGAs within Ebira territory at the time of research for this monograph. But after a military coup in January 1984, the number of local government areas was reduced to two—Okene and Okehi, the two created by an earlier military government before the civilian rule of 1979–1983.

The degree of mutual intelligibility among the various dialects of Ebira has not been established, but I have difficulty in understanding speakers of other dialects.

In recent years a number of political changes have taken place and are still taking place in the country as a whole. In 1967 the country, which formerly consisted of four regions and a number of provinces, was reconstituted into a twelve-state structure by the then federal military government headed by General Yakubu Gowon. In 1976 the total number of states of the Federation was increased to nineteen, and in the same year another important political reform created local government areas within each of those nineteen states. Thus the old Divisions within Provinces came to be replaced by local government areas and it was in the same way that the old Igbirra Division in Kabba Province, which was the home of the Ebira people, came to be divided into its six LGAs between 1976 and 1981. It is not yet clear what further structural changes may occur in the country with the new military government headed by General Muhammadu Buhari.

1.2 The Language Name

The name *Igbirra* was used for many years to refer to the language and the people. This spelling of the name came about largely due to historical developments and contact with Yoruba, a major dominant language neighbor to Ebira. However, the people themselves call their language Ebira [èbìrà] and refer to themselves as Anebira [anébìrà] 'people of Ebira'. In 1974, a strong ethnic organization known as Ebira People's Association (EPA) formally changed the language name from *Igbirra* to *Ebira* and published this change in the Nigerian daily newspapers. Writers in the language and about the language have gradually changed to the correct name, *Ebira,* which I am using for the language in this study because any proper synchronic linguistic study has to give an objective account of what the speakers of a language say about their language.

1.3 Neighboring Languages

The main neighboring languages of Ebira are Yoruba to the west, Igala to the east, Edo to the south, and Nupe to the north (see Map 3). Among these, Yoruba seems to have had more influence than others on Ebira in various ways. For example, Western education and missionary activities spread from the Yoruba people to the Ebiras. The first schools among the Ebiras were established by the Church Missionary Society (CMS) and the Roman Catholic Mission. Most teachers in these schools in the early days were Yorubas, and Yoruba was the medium of instruction in the schools for the first three years. This is one reason why a number of educated Ebiras

Introduction 3

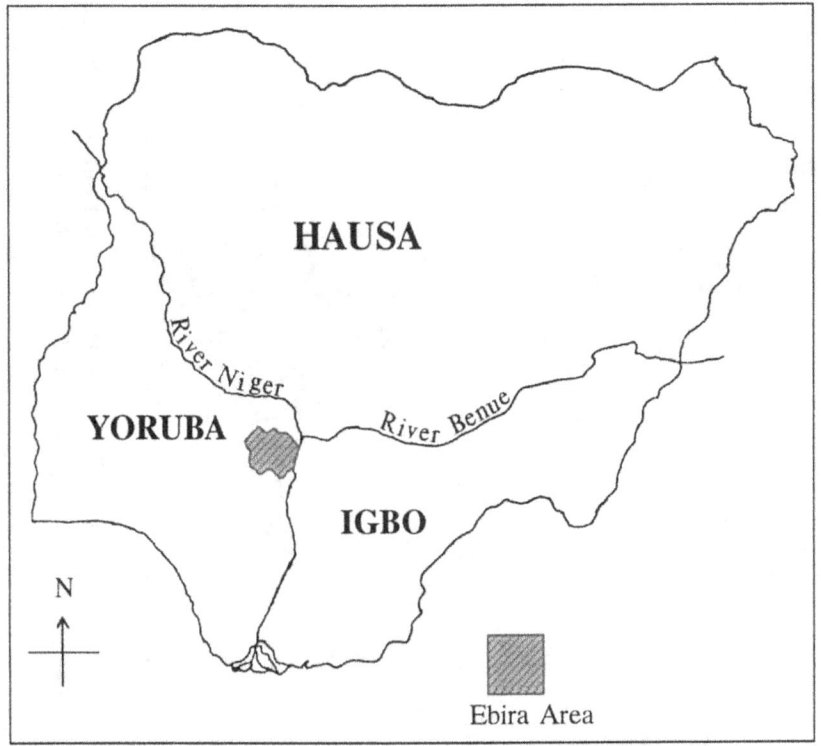

Map 1. Nigeria showing the Ebira area and Nigeria's major languages.

Scale: 0   60   120 ML

Source: Studies in Nigerian Languages No. 5
         Summer Institute of Linguistics (S.I.L.), Ghana, 1976

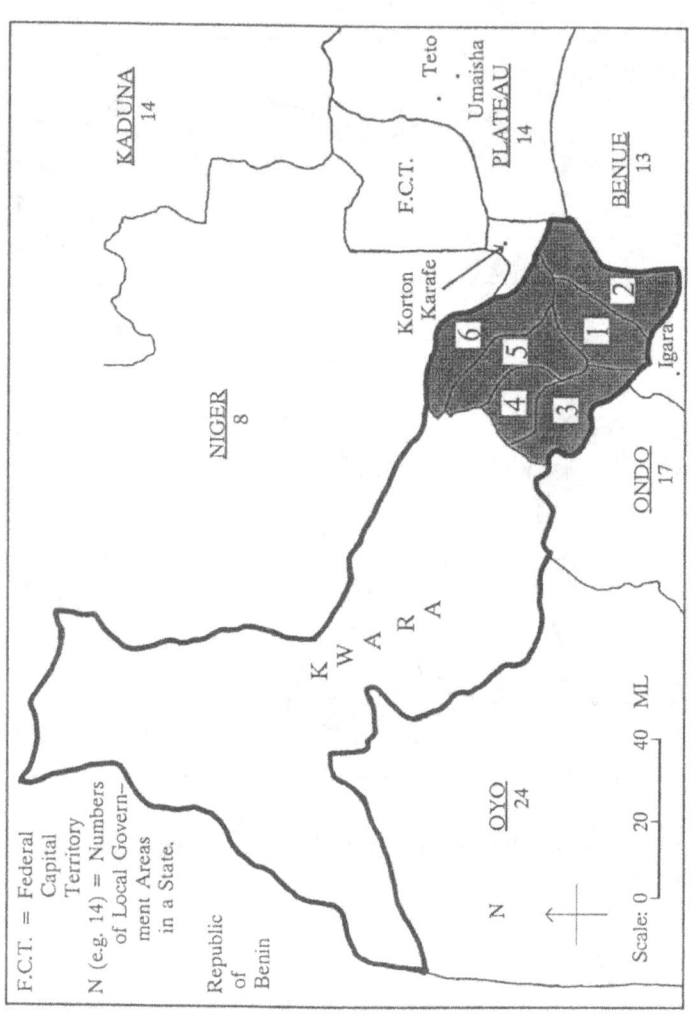

Map 2. KWARA state showing the six LGA's (shaded) of the Ebira area, the neighboring states (underlined), and other local dialect towns of the Ebira language.

Source: Nigeria in Maps; Hodder and Stoughton, London, 1982

Introduction

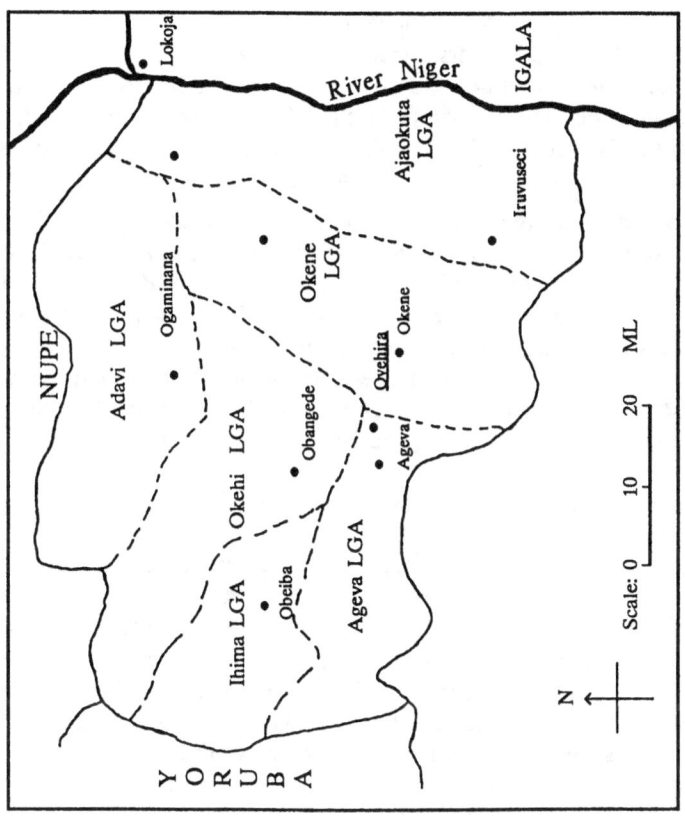

Map 3. Ebira area showing the six LGA's, the main towns, and the major neighboring languages.

Source: Ageva LGA maps of Kwara state and local governments. Ageva, 1982.

are bilingual. It was only in the third or fourth year of primary instruction that English was introduced as the medium of instruction. I myself went through this system in my early days of formal education.

Another example of Yoruba influence on Ebira is in the area of agriculture. The Ebira area is small, considering the population of the language community. The land is hilly and mountainous. Large quantities of iron were discovered in the hills in the late sixties, leading to the establishment of the Ajaokuta Steel Industry by the federal government in the seventies. But the Ebira people as a whole are farmers. Since their native land is so rocky and too small to meet their requirements, a large number of them are forced to look for arable land elsewhere, mainly in the Yoruba area. Through this contact they naturally acquire the Yoruba language, so there are some bilingual Ebiras among the uneducated folk as well.

Wherever they may be the Ebiras keep in constant touch with their homeland. The farmer maintains two homes: one is in Ebira native land where he keeps his family; the other is a temporary one (usually a hut) in an alien land where he does his farming. Educated Ebiras who may have employment outside the homeland return to their homes and families as frequently as possible. Much of their property is usually kept in their Ebira homes, not where they are employed. The people's attachment to their homeland is a major factor in keeping the language alive and dynamic.

1.4 Language Family Affiliation

Ebira belongs to the Kwa Niger-Congo family group according to the classification of African languages by Greenberg (1963, 1970), who lists Nupe, Gbari, Igbirra, and Gade as subgroup (d) under Kwa. Note that these are not necessarily the immediate geographical neighbors of Ebira. (See Map 3 and §1.3). In a later regrouping of Nigerian languages, Hansford et al. (1976) separate Ebira from Nupe, Gbari, and Gade and set up Ebira as a sub-subgroup on its own. This group would comprise the main dialect of Ebira and only one of the local dialects (the Igara) of the three mentioned in §1.1. Hansford et al. still classify Ebira as belonging to the Kwa subgroup of the Niger-Congo family.

Many languages of the West African coast belong to the Kwa group which spreads well beyond the borders of Nigeria. Some of the important members of this family, like the Akan languages of Ghana; Ewe, spoken in parts of Ghana, Togo, and Benin; Yoruba in southwest Nigeria; and Igbo in the eastern part of Nigeria, have received a great deal of attention in linguistic studies.

Introduction

1.5 Literature Survey

It is only in recent years that attention has been given to lesser-known Nigerian languages like Ebira. The earlier records and mention of these MINORITY languages were made by missionaries and British administrative officers. Some of those who mentioned Ebira in their records and works incude the following:

- Clarke (1848) was a Baptist missionary who published a collection of vocabularies of African languages. He includes two varieties of Igbirra vocabulary in his collection. This is the earlist record of Igbirra dialects.
- Koelle (1854) mentions three varieties of Igbirra: Opanda, Igu, and Ebira-Hima; he lists about 200 vocabulary items and about 40 phrases for each.
- Cust (1883) records two dialects of Igbirra: Panda and Hima.
- Johnson and Christaller (1886) published a collection of vocabularies of the Niger and the Gold Coast languages. It is said that Johnson translated the Psalms and the Catechism into the Igbirra language.
- Thomas (1914) mentions Igara as a dialect of Igbirra and includes a wordlist of 31 items of Igbirra.
- Westermann and Bryan (1952) include Igbirra as one of the three dialect clusters of the Nupe group. They list four dialects for Igbirra: Igbirra-Panda, Igbirra-Ihima, Igbirra-Egu, and Igara.
- Brown (1958) repeats the four Igbirra dialects listed by Westermann and Bryan and adds a note that all the dialects of Igbirra are mutually intelligible.

It can be observed from the above that references to the Igbirra language in the works listed are very general and extremely limited.

The literature about the Ebira language from the sixties and later differs markedly from the earlier contributions. It was from the sixties that specific linguistic articles on the language began to appear, starting from Greenberg (1963), who surveyed languages of Africa and classified them from massive word lists. His classification of Ebira under Kwa is generally accepted as standard.

The first technical linguistic paper on the phonology of Ebira was "Igbirra Notes and Word-List" by Ladefoged (1964). In this paper Ladefoged introduces the vowel harmony system of the language. (See footnote 1, below, page 23.)

The next significant linguistic investigation is by Hans-Jürgen Scholz of the Summer Institute of Linguistics. Scholz stayed in the Ebira area from 1973 to 1976. He developed a practical orthography for the language, published some literacy and religious pamphlets, and supervised the translation of the Ebira New Testament. His main linguistic publication is *Igbirra Phonology (1976)* published by S.I.L. in its Language Data microfiche series No.7. There are a number of inaccuracies and semantic misrepresentations in the microfiche publication. My critique of the phonology is forthcoming.

1.6 The Present Study

The above summary shows that to date no linguistic description and analysis of the Ebira language exists. There has been a growing desire and interest among Ebira people to preserve their culture and identity by broadening the use of their language. The federal government of Nigeria formulated language policies in 1977 which encouraged the use of indigenous languages for education and social purposes. Linguists and scholars in language-related disciplines are searching for sound descriptions of less-known languages on which further research and work could be based.

My aim is to present an adequate description of the verbal piece in Ebira. The verbal piece is selected for this study because it is the most phonologically, morphologically, and grammatically complex unit in Ebira, and therefore offers the widest scope for the descriptive analysis of the language. The term VERBAL PIECE is used to refer to the verb word, the verbal phrase, the verbal clause, and the verbal group of various types. These pieces, which are described in chapters 4 to 6, are units for which the grammatical categories of mood, tense, polarity, person, and number can be stated. Other pieces, like nominal forms for which these categories do not apply, are described only to the extent necessary for explanation of a particular verbal piece.

Ebira is a VERB-CENTERED language. An accurate description of the verbal system covers the core of the grammar of the language. As F.R. Palmer (1965:1) remarks:

> The most difficult part of any language is usually the part that deals with the verb. Learning a language is to a very large degree learning how to operate the verbal forms of that language, and, except in the cases of those that are related historically, the patterns and structure of the verb in each language seem to differ considerably from those in every other language.

My description of the Ebira verbal piece is based on my personal knowledge of the language, tape recordings of plays, folk narratives, and conversations of other native speakers of Ebira. The form of Ebira described is the spoken form, since there are very few written texts in the language as yet.

1.7 The Theoretical Basis of the Study

Since this is a general survey and description of a language, I have not rigidly followed one particular theoretical framework. Nevertheless, I find the prosodic framework developed by J.R. Firth (1948) and others convenient in describing the phonology of Ebira, because Ebira exhibits a vowel harmony system where phonetic details of the speech stream operate beyond individual elements of a word or a phrase. Further still, some important syntagmatic relations and functions operative in Ebira speech are simply economically described in terms of prosodies and prosodic elements of structure (see §§2.3 and 5.10).

I also find the syntagmatic approach, used by John T. Bendor-Samuel (1961) in describing the Jebero verbal piece, useful in establishing the grammatical hierarchy for levels of units in the Ebira verbal piece (see §4.1).

In describing in detail elements of the grammatical categories of the hierarchy, I find J. Carnochan's (1970) structure in "Categories of the Verbal Piece in Bachama" extremely useful.

I believe that one needs to be eclectic in approach to a new language in general description; otherwise he runs the risk of subjecting the language to certain set theories which may not explain some basic phenomena that make the language what it is. It should be stressed that the aim is neither to vindicate nor to invalidate the above theoretical models. I only employ them as fully as possible to explain a vital grammatical aspect of Ebira phenomena, the verbal piece.

2 Phonology

2.1 The Syllable Structure

The smallest units of structure in the phonology of Ebira are consonants (C), vowels (V) and tones (T). The structure of the syllable (s) can be described in terms of these three elements.

Every syllable has a vowel or a syllabic nasal (n) as its nucleus. In CV syllables the C is a marginal element.

Tone is a distinctive identificational feature of the syllable. Every syllable bears tone which is evinced by the pitch of the voiced parts, regularly carried by the vowel or the syllabic nasal.

Thus the nucleus of the syllable always carries one of the three level tones or one of the two kinetic tones of the language.

Tones on the syllables are marked as follows:

High tone	/´/
Mid tone	unmarked
Low tone	/`/
High-falling tone	/ˆ/
Low-rising tone	/ˇ/

Tone is described in detail in §2.6.

Ebira has three syllable types: V plus tone, n plus tone, and CV plus tone.

Syllable type 1

Syllable type 1 has the general formula $s_1 \rightarrow T(V)$.

Tone is looked on here as being a prosodic element of the syllable as a whole, and the structure is therefore rewritten as T(V). Syllable type 1 consists of a vowel as nucleus plus tone.

ô/ộ[1]	V̂	a vowel syllable preverb denoting person and number, as in the first two examples below, meaning 'he, she or it'.
ô ré	V̂ CV́	'he saw'
ộ mẹ̀	V̂ CV̀	'he did'
òzè	V̀CV̀	'a road'
ọyi	VCV	'sun'
eehí	VVCV́	'home'
irehí	VCVCV́	'house'
òòhu	V̀V̀CV	'twenty'
ọnẹé	VCVV́	'woman'
ọdáa	VCV́V	'law'
àtààhù	V̀CV̀V̀CV̀	'ankle'
etéèsù	VCV́V̀CV̀	'floor'
evìnà	VCV́CV̀	'water yam'
oríhì	VCV́CV̀	'teen-age girl'

As illustrated above, the V syllables may occur initially, medially, or finally in the phonological word. In grammatically complex words, up to three V syllables may occur in succession word initially, and up to two may occur in succession word medially or finally. For example:

àáavẹ́, ọ̀ hị̀ ịkẹ̀kẹ́	'if he is coming, he should buy a bicycle'
àpáápà	'maize, corn'
ùsùú	'anklet (very special ornament)'

More examples of geminate vowel sequences are described in §2.2.

Syllable type 2

Syllable type 2 has the general formula $s_2 \rightarrow T(N)$.

Syllable type 2 is similar to syllable type 1 in having a single segmental element; but it is a syllabic nasal, and not a vowel, that carries the tone and is the nucleus. All type 2 syllables are followed in the same word by a CV syllable. They do not occur word finally and therefore none of the syllabic nasals ever carry either of the two kinetic tones of the language, since kinetic tones occur only on word-final syllables. The articulation of the syllabic nasal is homorganic with the consonant that immediately follows it.

---

[1]Ebira is a diatic language where a noun and a pronoun preverb both refer to the same subject.

Phonology

ǹdá	ŃCV́	'father'	(alveolar)
ɲ̀ɲá	ŃCV́	'mother'	(palatal)
àm̀pò	V̀ǸCV̀	'a bag'	(bilabial)
ihìǹnà	V̀CV́ǸCV̀	'nine'	(alveolar)
ójíŋgà	V́CV́ŃCV̀	'a digger'	(velar)
caŋgadaa	CVNCVCVV	'very wide and flat'	(velar)

Syllable type 3

Syllable type 3 has the general formula $s_3 \rightarrow T(CV)$.

Syllable type 3 consists of margin C plus nucleus V plus tone. For example:

hí	CV́	'to call'
sì	CV̀	'to look for'
ne	CV	'to throw'
hèré	CV̀CV́	'to vomit'
kùrú	CV̀CV́	'to tie a knot'
sáàsá	CV́V̀CV́	'to follow'
póóró	CV́V́CV́	'always, for a long time'

Monosyllabic verbs and the first syllable of polysyllabic verbs are all of structure CV.

Ebira is an open-syllable language; i.e., it has no syllables with final –C. Syllable types 1, 2 and 3 are combined in organized structures to form words and other grammatical constructions. Most words in the language consist of one to four syllables; only a few consist of more than four.

Summary of one to four syllable structures

The structure of words of one to four syllables in the language may be summarized as follows:

Monosyllabic	V	N-	CV
Disyllabic	VV	VCV	NCV
	CVV	CVCV	
Trisyllabic	VVV	VVCV	VNCV
	VCVV	VCVCV	CVVCV
	CVCVCV	CVNCV	
Tetrasyllabic	VVCVCV	VNCVCV	VCVVCV
	VCVNCV	VCVCVCV	VCVCVV
	CVCVCVV	CVCVCVCV	

Labialization as a feature in the syllable

Labialization as a phonemic feature of the consonant within the syllable occurs with the fricative consonants and two velar consonants in just the words cited as examples in this section. Labialization as a phonemic feature signals meaning contrasts with pure consonant phonemes in content words such as nouns and verbs. Contrasting pairs are given in cases where they are found to illustrate the contrast between syllables with a labial feature and syllables without one. Labialization is symbolized by *w* following a consonant.

/v/	vwọ̀	C^wV̀	'to cook flour meal'
	vọ	CV	'to cut animal meat into big pieces'
/s/	swẹ́	C^wV́	'to take iron blade from hoe handle'
	sé	CV́	'to chop off grass'
	óswe	V́C^wV	'water spring near a hill'
	òsé	V̀CV́	'wife'
	swe	C^wV	'to start weaving a basket or mat; to initiate an idea/proposal'
	swé	C^wV́	'to cough'
	ọswẹ́	VC^wV́	'ankle ornament'
	òsẹ̀	V̀CV̀	'alligator pepper'
	swá	C^wV́	'to be smooth, to be slippery'
/z/	zwè	C^wV̀	'to run'
	zé	CV́	'to be enough'
	zwọ́	C^wV́	'to be scarce'
/h/	èhwẹ	V̀C^wV	'pieces of dried yam'
	ehẹ	VCV	'world, life'
	uhwẹ	VC^wV	'spirit, breath, life'
	uhwó	VC^wV́	'barn'
	ùhwò	V̀C^wV̀	'knife'
	ùúhwe	V̀V́C^wV	'hen'
	ùhwóọ	V̀C^wV́V	'tomorrow'
/k/	kwọ̀	C^wV̀	'to grind'
	kọ́	CV́	'to learn' (possibly a loan-word from Yoruba or vice versa)
	ùkwò	V̀C^wV̀	'soap'
	ụ́kộ	V́CV̂	'big, hollow stone place where raw palm oil is extracted from boiled palm fruit'
	kwòrò	C^wV̀CV̀	'to be thin, to iron clothes'
	kwákwaa	C^wV́C^wVV	'exclamation for happiness or surprise'
	kwékwee	C^wV́C^wVV	'exclamation for sympathy'
/ŋ/	ŋwẹ	C^wV	'to spin cotton wool'
	ŋẹ	CV	'an abusive word for a child having a big head'

Phonology

ŋwà	CʷV̀	'to loosen or undo'
ŋa	CV	'adverbial intensifier for shooting the arrow to hit the target straight and strongly'
aŋwẹ́	VCʷV	'oil'
àŋwà (hí)	V̀CʷV̀ (CV́)	'fear'
oŋwẹ	VCʷV	'voice'
òŋwiŋwịí	V̀CʷVCʷV̀V́	'the sixth generation of children in a family tree'

Notice that in all these examples the labialization feature is always followed by a nonclose vowel (a, o, e or ẹ) except the last word which is a very rare vocabulary item.

Labialization is phonetically manifested by lip rounding with slight protruding of both lips.

An alternative analysis would be to set up six consonant phonemes, *vw*, *sw*, *zw*, *hw*, *kw* and *ŋw*, in addition to *v*, *s*, *z*, *h*, *k* and *ŋ*. For descriptive economy, however, labialization is treated as a feature of the syllable.

Yet another suggestion would be to analyze the labialization as a vowel. This analysis is rejected because:

(a) the phonetic pronunciation is different from any other vowel element in the language.

For *kọ́* and *vọ* there is lip rounding, which can be related to the rounded back vowel, while in *kwọ̀* and *vwọ̀* there is additional closer lip rounding which cannot easily be related to the -*ọ*, nor can the rounding for the consonant articulation in the other examples be related at all to the following vowels, which are *e*, *ẹ*, and *a*, all unrounded nonclose vowels.

(b) The labialized syllables have only one tone each, and therefore cannot be considered to involve any vowel sequences.

Palatalization as a feature in the syllable

Palatalization as a feature within the syllable occurs only with the glottal fricative phoneme /h/ and is found in just a few nominal words of VCV or VCVCV syllable structure. The contrast between the palatalized glottal fricative and the pure glottal fricative is exemplified below. Palatalization is symbolized by *y* following the glottal fricative and *y* following the C- in the syllable structure.

/h/	ịhyè	VCʸV̀	'teeth ridge, alveolar'
	ehẹ	VCV	'world, life'
	ịhyèrè	V̀CV̀CʸV̀	'feces'
	òhérẹ	V̀CV́CV	'male name'

i̱hyámá	V̀Cʸv́CV́	'louse, lice'
òháma	V̀CV́CV	'an imitator'
i̱hyọ́ọ́	V̀Cʸv́V	'then, a few days ago'
i̱ri̱hyà	V̀CV̀ʸCV̀	'hernia of the testicles'
íhyénhyere	V́ʸCV́Ń ʸCVCV	'hedgehog'
i̱hyẹ́mi̱hyẹmẹ̀	V́ʸCV́CV́ʸCVCV̀	'sweet potato'

The seven words listed above are the only words found within the corpus of this study that manifest this very rare syllable feature.

The arguments for not setting up additional phonemes for labialization advanced in the preceding section hold for palatalization. Therefore *hy* is not set up as a separate phoneme.

Labialization and palatalization occur across morpheme or word boundaries under specific phonological conditions. These are discussed in §§3.2 and 3.3, with regard to these features being prosodic elements of the syllable.

2.2 The Vowel Phonemes

Ebira has nine vowel phonemes. It is possible to cite many words as lexical evidence for each phoneme established. To keep this section from becoming unnecessarily long, the following list provides only sufficient data necessary for background understanding of further grammatical analysis of the verbal piece in the chapters that follow.

/i/ [i] Close front vowel with lips spread.
It has almost Cardinal 1 quality.
    hí   'to weave'
    iyá   'pounded yam'

/i̱/ [i̱] A front vowel between close and half-close
and with lips spread; it is slightly retracted.
    hi̱   'to call'
    i̱tà   'cloth'

/e/ [e] Half-close front vowel with lips spread and
rather more open than Cardinal 2.
    ré   'to see'
    ezí   'children'

/ẹ/ [ẹ] Half-open front vowel with lips neutral to
spread, and rather more open than Cardinal 3.
    bẹ́   'to carve'
    ẹvú 'goat'

Phonology

/a/ [a] Open central vowel with lips spread.
  pá 'to train'
  ano̞ 'salt'

/o̞/ [o̞] Half-open to open back vowel with lips open rounded.
  tó̞ 'to chew'
  o̞cí 'stick'

/o/ [o] Half-close back vowel with close rounded lips, and rather more open than Cardinal 7.
  po 'to mix with liquid'
  ohi 'broom'

/u̞/ [u̞] A back rounded vowel between close and half-close with lips close rounded. It is slightly advanced.
  hú̞ 'to boil'
  u̞pà 'skin, hide'

/u/ [u] Close back vowel with lips close rounded. It has almost Cardinal 8 quality.
  hú 'to drink'
  uné 'gazelle'

All these nine vowel phonemes occur word initially, word medially, and word finally in the language. Each of the vowels can also occur in sequences of two vowels in a word or a sentence.

Geminate vowel sequences

Phonetically long vowels that occur in Ebira are treated as sequences of the same vowel, VV and VVV, phonologically and morphologically. I interpret double-length vowels as sequences of two vowels for the reasons given in this section.

Two identical vowels can occur initially, medially, or finally in an Ebira word. They are not the manifestation of a length feature, because each of the identical vowels may bear a different tone; and because tone is a distinctive feature of the syllable (§2.1), a geminate vowel sequence spreads over two syllables. All possible two-syllable tone combinations allowed by the language can occur on geminate vowels in all positions. For tone analysis, see §2.6.

There are no sequences of nonidentical vowels within a word. The syllable of the second identical vowel in a word can be regarded as a schwa (ə-) syl-lable as the two vowels do not constitute separate alternances. J. Carnochan ([1960]1970:224), discussing a similar occurrence in Igbo, states:

> The vowel sound in the second syllable of each example is the same as in the final syllable; together they constitute one alternance.... In this syllable I recognize a syllabic: ə. This V-ə phonological notation indicates the interdependence of the syllables and correlates with hearing the same vowel sound in both syllables.

Carnochan's Igbo examples have a CVCV syllable structure. In the Ebira examples the vowels are contiguous. However, the two languages manifest a structural schwasyllable prosody. (See chapter 3 for full discussion of syntactic prosodies in Ebira.)

Initial geminate vowel sequences, V-ə. In the following examples, double vowels are written for two-vowel sequences in phonetic representation while ə-syllable is written for the second vowel in the syllable structure representation. A contrasting pair with a single vowel in the same position is given below each word except where one cannot be found:

ùúhwẹ́	VəCV	[_ ‾ ─]	'hen'
uhwẹ́	VCV	[─ ‾]	'moon'
ààhẹ̀	VəCV	[_ _ _]	'play, drama'
ahẹ́	VCV	[─ ‾]	'song'
óóhẹ	V́əCV	[‾ ‾ ─]	'free of charge'
ohẹ́	VCV́	[─ ‾]	'a pillar of a house'
ọ̀ọ̀ṇị	V̀əCV	[_ _ ─]	'one'
ọ̀ṇị́	V̀CV́	[_ ‾]	'mother'
èèva	V̀əCV	[_ _ ─]	'two'
eva	VCV	[─ ─]	'oracle'
èèhí	V̀əCV́	[_ _ ‾]	'five'
ehí	VCV́	[─ ‾]	'sweat'

All Ebira basic numbers when counting have initial double vowels. These are:

ọ̀ọ̀ṇị	'one'	èèva	'two'	èètá	'three'	èènà	'four'
èèhí	'five'	èèwú	'ten'	òòhu	'twenty'		

Medial geminate vowel sequences, -Və-.

àpáapà	V̀CV́əCV̀	[_ ‾ ─ _]	'maize'
apápa	VCV́CV	[─ ‾ ─]	'bean bread'
àtàáhù	V̀CV̀əCV̀	[_ _ ‾ _]	'ankle'

Phonology

àtàhú	V̀CV̀CV́	[_ _ ¯]	'kernel of palm fruit'
etèèsù	VCV́əCV̀	[_ ¯ _ _]	'floor'
íkûzà	V́CV̂əCV̀	[¯ ¯ _ _]	'cow peas'

Words having geminate vowel sequences medially are rare in the language.

Final geminate vowel sequences, -Və.

onóọ	VCV́ə	[_ ¯ _]	'that' (demonstrative)
ọ̀nọ̀	V̀CV̀	[_ _]	'warning'
enée	VCV́ə	[_ ¯ _]	'those' (subj. demonstrative)
ènè	V̀CV́	[_ ¯]	'who' (question word, relative pronoun)
òmumùú	V̀CVCV̀V́	[_ _ _ ¯]	'fontanel'
òsisíí	V̀CVCV̀V́	[_ _ _ ¯]	'a hole in the lower part of the compound wall for water outlet'

Only two words of more than three syllables have been found in the language having a geminate vowel sequence word finally. These are the two words ending the list above and they seem to be onomatopoeic words.

Consonant deletion in VV words

Some words develop VV elements from the deletion of an intervocalic consonant. These words still maintain the same number of syllables and the same tone pattern even when the medial consonant is deleted. The two versions of the same word may be in current use without any change or with very slight change in semantic connotation. Words of this pattern are extremely limited in the language.

It is the consideration of such different pronunciations for the same item, with and without the consonant, that further confirms the treatment elsewhere of long phonetic vowels as sequences of two V elements phonologically:

irehí (house)	or	eehí	VəCV́	[_ _ ¯]	'home'
àwùrú	or	ààrú	V̀əCV́	[_ _ ¯]	'gown'
àvàbá	or	ààbá	V̀əCV́	[_ _ ¯]	'all'

A few constructions of reduplicated forms, in which the medial consonant is /r/ and the first and second vowels are identical, manifest consonant deletion and the development of medial VV sequence in the first part of the reduplicated form:

kerekere	CVCVCVCV	[– – – –]	'most' (the superlative attributive)
or			
keekere	CVəCVCV	[– – – –]	
dèrèdèrè	CV̀CV̀CV̀CV̀	[_ _ _ _]	
or			'to be thin'
dèèdèrè	CV̀əCV̀CV̀	[_ _ _ _]	

Both forms of the words are in current use also.

Loan-words in Ebira

Loan-words assimilated into Ebira conform to the syllable structure of the language. Ebira has no stressed syllables as English does (indicated below by ' preceding a stressed syllable). VV sequences with high tone followed by low tone occur where there is a stressed syllable in the English words that enter the language. Furthermore, an epenthetic vowel is added initially to any English nominal having an initial consonant because all nominals except bound pronoun objects in Ebira start with a vowel. Another epenthetic vowel is added finally to any English word having a closed syllable because Ebira is an open-syllable language. This means that some one-syllable English words may have three or four syllables when assimilated into Ebira, as shown in the examples below:

ENGLISH	*John*	['jɔn]	CVC	
EBIRA	*Ijoonu*	[ijóònù]	VCV́V̀əCV̀	[– – – –]
ENGLISH	*police*	[pə'lis]	CVCVC	
EBIRA	*iporiisi*	[ìpòrîìsì]	V̀CV̀CV́V̀əCV̀	[_ _ ‾ _ _]
ENGLISH	*comb*	['kouᵘm]	CVC	
EBIRA	*ikoomu*	[ikóòmù]	VCV́V̀əCV̀	[– ‾ _ _]
ENGLISH	*tea*	['ti]	CV	
EBIRA	*itii*	[itîì]	VCV́V̀	[– ‾ _]

Generally speaking, phonetically LONG VOWELS are rare in the language. The above data illustrate all the environments where geminate vowel sequences occur.

The word *tao*

There is only one word with a sequence of non-identical vowels found in Ebira. It is a word which expresses general greetings.

tàó	CV̀V́	[_ ‾]	'hello'

Phonology

The word has an alternative form:

tàn^wàó CV̀CV́V́   [_ _ ¬]   'hello'

The alternative form is normally used by the older people, but *tàó* is the more common form and is in frequent use. It is such a common and frequent greeting among the people that neighboring tribes refer to us as "Ebira-tao". There are no other examples in Ebira of this final *o* in greeting. (Greetings usually end in *e*, though in the neighboring Yoruba language many greetings end in *o*.)

YORUBA	EBIRA	
ẹ pẹlẹ o	tao nịnị e	'hello to you' (pl)
ẹ ku isẹ o	akọ́rọ́ nịnị e	'greeting at work'
ẹ kuabọ o	ɲásè̩ nịnị e	'welcome'

(Note: *nịnị* is a plural particle in Ebira.)

The status of /u/ and /u̩/ as variants of /i/ and /i̩/ in word-initial and word-medial positions

/u/ and /u̩/ fluctuate with /i/ and /i̩/ initially in lexical items where the second vowel is /u/ or /u̩/ respectively. The same speaker may use either form.

itù	and	ùtù	'ceiling'
ikù	and	ùkù	'scorpion'
isú	and	usú	'house rat'
inú	and	unú	'bush rat'
ihú	and	uhú	'seed'
i̩kù̩	and	ù̩kù̩	'disease, sickness'
itùtù	and	ùtùtù	'rubbish heap'
ihùhú	and	ùhùhú	'murmur'
igugu	and	ùgugu	'stump of a tree'
irùvú	and	ùrùvú	'toad'
irukú	and	urukú	'forest'
i̩ruka̩	and	u̩ruku̩	'farming'

It is only in initial position that *u* and *u̩* fluctuate with *i* and *i̩*. They contrast in all other positions. The above words are the only ones found in the data surveyed.

Charts of the vowel phonemes

I have listened to the recording of the cardinal vowels by Daniel Jones and have plotted Ebira vowels according to my perception of them in relation to the cardinal vowels.

(a) Traditional Cardinal Vowel Equivalent Chart

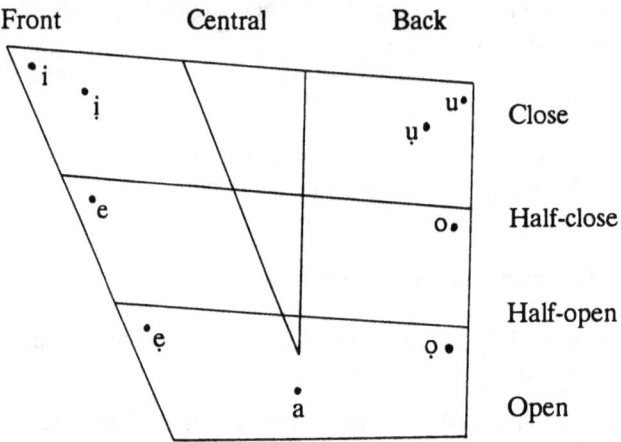

(b) Descriptive Vowel Chart

Lips	Front Spread	Central Neutral	Back Rounded
Close	i		u
Half-close	ị		ụ
Half-open	e		o
Open	ẹ 	a	ọ

Phonology

2.3 Vowel Harmony

The vowels of a language in which harmony[1] operates are usually in two groups. Various terms have been applied by linguists working on West African languages where vowel harmony operates to refer to the two groups. Some used the terms FORTIS and LENIS to refer to them. J. M. Stewart (1967) applied the terms advanced tongue root (+ATR) and unadvanced tongue root (-ATR) to refer to the two vowel harmony sets in the Akan language of Ghana which, like Ebira, belong to the Kwa language family.

In Ebira, however, I am using the simple terms HARMONIC VOWEL SET A and HARMONIC VOWEL SET B in my discussion of this topic.

The nine vowels of the language operate in two harmonic sets. These are:

Set A   *i e a o u*
Set B   *ị ẹ a ọ ụ*

The harmonic sets can be arranged as follows:

SET A	SET B	COMBINED SETS
i u	ị ụ	i u
e o	ẹ ọ	ị ụ
a	a	e o
		ẹ ọ
		a

The vowel /a/ is common to both sets, as shown above and in the following examples.

a-i	àyì	'measles'	íyá	'pounded yam'
a-ị	ayị	'flour'	ịpá	'calabash, cup'
a-e	àgé	'a jug'	eebàà	'yes, indeed'
a-ẹ	ahẹ́	'song'	ẹ̀há	'kind of plant'
			àjà	'a special feather'
a-ọ	anọ́	'salt'	ọhá	'spear'
a-o	akó	'a cup'		
a-ụ	àkụ́	'guinea corn'	ụ̀kà	'food of yam flour'
a-u	àmù	'a cap'		

---

[1] Ladefoged (1964) first discusses Ebira vowel harmony in his article "Igbirra Notes and Word-List". He introduces the vowels /ị/ and /ụ/. He also mentions (1968:37) Ebira vowel harmony in his book *A Phonetic Study of West African Languages*. Ladefoged's treatment of the topic is general and typological. Further research has suggested that a more detailed description will throw additional light on the analysis of Ebira.

The vowel harmony system of Ebira manifests itself in the two major lexical word classes of the language, the nominal class and the verbal class.

The nominal class

The nominal class is congruent with the grammatical noun, pronoun, adjective, demonstrative, numeral, and temporal.

Words of the nominal class always have an initial V syllable as distinct from those of the verbal class which always have an initial C. The initial vowel appears to be a remnant of a noun class prefix, but in the present-day language very little of the noun class system remains. There are just a few examples of nouns with contrastive singular and plural prefixes. These comprise:

SINGULAR		PLURAL	
òzà	'a person'	àzà	'people'
oneẹ́	'a woman'	aneẹ́	'women'
onorú	'a man'	anorú	'men'
òzoga	'a visitor'	àzoga	'visitors'
òhíní	'co-wife'	èhíní	'co-wives'
ozí	'child'	ezí	'children'
òsé	'wife'	èsé	'wives'

Note that all of these nouns refer to persons. These few nouns with a relation of o/o as a prefix to the singular and a/e to the plural are reminiscent of the o/a personal class of nouns in some Bantu languages. (See Wolf 1971; Hyman 1980.) This is not a typical system of pluralization in present Ebira. (See §4.8.)

Nominal words can be formed from harmony vowels of either set A or set B. But vowels from the two sets are not normally found in the same word apart from /a/ which belongs to both sets.

Set A: *i, e, o, u, a* in nominal words.

i-i	ìzì	'bambara nuts'
i-e	ìze	'grass cutter (big bush rodent)'
i-o	ìsó	'nail'
i-u	isu	'house rat'
i-a	iya	'pounded yam'

Phonology

e-i	eyí	'eye'
e-e	ècè	'wine'
e-o	ètò	'arrangement'
e-u	ekú	'masquerade'
e-a	eebàà	'yes, indeed'
o-i	oyí	'thief'
o-e	òzè	'road'
o-o	òbó	'rope'
o-u	òwú	'cotton'
o-a	—	—
u-i	ùjì	'basket'
u-e	uye	'meat'
u-o	útô	'cowrie shell'
u-u	ùrù	'mushroom'
u-a	—	—
a-i	ayì	'measles'
a-e	àgé	'a jug'
a-o	ako	'a calabash cup'
a-u	ákù	'inner room'
a-a	àbà	'yam heaps'

The table below gives the summary of set A cooccurence of vowels in words of VCV pattern.

		2ND VOWEL				
		i	e	o	u	a
1ST VOWEL	i	x	x	x	x	x
	e	x	x	x	x	x
	o	x	x	x	x	
	u	x	x	x	x	
	a	x	x	x	x	x

There are no lexical words like *oka and *uga in the language.

Set B: i̩, e̩, o̩, u̩, a in nominal words.

i̩-i̩	ihi̩	'justification'
i̩-e̩	iné̩	'stomach'
i̩-o̩	iŋò̩	'weighing machine, scale'
i̩-u̩	ikù̩	'sickness, disease'
i̩-a	irá	'fire'

ẹ-ị	ẹyị	'hair'
ẹ-ẹ	ẹhẹ	'world, life'
ẹ-ọ	ẹdọ	'antelope'
ẹ-ụ	ẹwụ	'snake'
ẹ-a	ẹpà	'root'
ọ-ị	ọcị́	'stick, tree'
ọ-ẹ	ọhẹ́	'pillar of a house'
ọ-ọ	ọpọ́	'mask for masquerade'
ọ-ụ	ọkụ́	'firewood'
ọ-a	ọ̀pà	'arrow'
ụ-ị	ụhị́	'fable'
ụ-ẹ	ụnẹ	'locust bean'
ụ-ọ	ụ̀nọ	'cow'
ụ-ụ	ụtụ́	'message, errand'
ụ-a	ụ̀bà	'vulture'
a-ị	àrị́	'fishhook'
a-ẹ	ajẹ	'egg'
a-ọ	anọ́	'salt'
a-ụ	àgụ̀	'smell'
a-a	àtà	'testicles'

The table below summarizes set B cooccurrence of vowels in words of VCV pattern.

	2ND VOWEL				
	ị	ẹ	ọ	ụ	a
ị	x	x	x	x	x
ẹ	x	x	x	x	x
ọ	x	x	x	x	x
ụ	x	x	x	x	x
a	x	x	x	x	x

1ST VOWEL

All set B vowels can cooccur in VCV word combinations. This shows that set B has a wider occurrence and distribution in the language, and if it was advantageous to apply the concept MARKEDNESS to vowel harmony in Ebira then set B could be considered as unmarked and set A, marked.

Nominal words of more than two syllables. The vowel harmony system operates also in nouns of three, four, or more syllables.

Phonology

Set A: *i, e, o, u, a*

i- - -	*ihihìnè*	'ants'
e- - -	*éhepo*	'a kind of yam'
o- - -	*òkùkú*	'an imaginary being'
u- - -	*ukere*	'wooden door'
a- - -	*akúkù*	'some kind of vegetable'

Set B: *i̩, e̩, o̩, u̩, a*

i̩- - -	*i̩so̩vo̩*	'sacrifice'
e̩- - -	*e̩cúku̩*	'bone'
o̩- - -	*ògèdè*	'banana'
u̩- - -	*uko̩ro̩*	'work'
a- - -	*áru̩sà*	'walnut'

Compound and complex nominal words. There are a few instances where vowels from set A and vowels from set B occur in the same nominal word. Words in this class are usually names of people or of places. As in other Kwa languages (especially Yoruba), most Ebira names for people or places are a combination of two or more words. Sometimes a name could be a whole sentence. In such cases it is possible to have sequences of set A and set B vowels in one name.

NAMES	UNDERLYING WORDS
[ohíe̩kú̩]	òhi + ire̩kú̩ leader + war 'captain of war'
[ezúré̩]	ezí + uré̩ children + algae 'the Algae clan'
[o̩mècè]	òmè + ècè maker + wine 'wine brewer'
[o̩ʃéyízá]	òsí + eyí + zá one who takes + eye + hold 'one who remembers'

Other words in the nominal class. All the words cited so far are nouns. As the nominal word class includes pronouns, adjectives, demonstratives, numerals, and temporals, a few examples of each are given to illustrate the vowel initial feature and vowel harmony common to all of them.

PRONOUN

1st person singular	èmi	'I'
2nd person singular	èwu	'you'
3rd person singular	oni	'he, she, it'
1st person plural	èyi	'we'
2nd person plural	èwu nini	'you'
3rd person plural	énini/éni	'they'

ADJECTIVE   DEMONSTRATIVE

ógodo	'long'	onóo	'that'	
ówéyi	'small, short'	onóni	'this'	
óbání	'big'	enée	'those'	
ónúru	'many'	enéni	'these'	

NUMERAL   TEMPORAL

òòni	'one'	ajíni	'today'	
èèva	'two'	èèri	'yesterday'	
èèwu	'ten'	ùhwóó	'tomorrow'	
òòhu	'twenty'	irayí	'year'	

The verbal class

The verbal class is congruent with the grammatical verb, adverb, and ideophone. All verbal words begin with a consonant.

Harmony span in the verb phrase. In the examples of nouns it is not possible to say that the first syllable controls the second, or vice versa, but when verbal phrases are examined it is clear that it is the vowel (or vowels) in the verb stem that governs the other vowels in the phrase, making for a vowel harmony unity over the verbal phrase. Thus, for example, the 3rd person singular pronoun has two pronunciations, /o/ and /o̩/, according to the vowel harmony set of the verb in the phrase.

ô sì	'he wants'	ô sí	'he takes'	
ô ré	'he sees'	ô mè	'he does'	
ô rò	'he thinks'	ô dó	'he gets'	
ô hú	'he drinks'	ô hú	'he boils'	
		ô dà	'he cuts'	

In the above verbal phrases, the vowel of the verb word determines whether it is the pronoun preverb /o/ or /o̩/ that precedes the word. In addition, the vowel of the verb also dominates the pronominal piece progressively within the vp. Examine the following:

Phonology

VOWEL SET A
ô ré é   'he saw it'
ô tò ó   'he arranged it'
ô pèhé é   'he winnowed it'
ô gono ò   'he praised him'

VOWEL SET B
ộ gé ẹ́   'he sewed it'
ộ họ̀ ọ́   'he asked him'
ộ há á   'he peeled it'
ộ họ̀kọ́ ọ́   'he rinsed it'
ộ càká á   'he broke it'

The harmony prosody operates from the verb word to contiguous syllables regressively and progressively. Harmony prosody is a syntagmatic feature that spreads over a unit of structure within the sentence. Carnochan ([1960]1970:224), in dealing with a similar phenomenon in Igbo, states:

> The initial syllable, the pronoun, in all these eight examples, is pronounced with a high vowel, the particular degree of closeness correlating with the vowel harmony of the example as a whole.

The only exceptions with regard to progressive harmony dominance concern the close vowels, *i, ị, u, ụ*. These close vowels operate slightly differently at morpheme or word junctions. When the final vowel of the verb is one of the four close vowels, the object pronominal piece is always the lowered close back vowel /ọ/.

VOWEL SET A
ô hí ọ́   'he wove it (cloth)'
ô hú ọ́   'he drank it'

VOWEL SET B
ộ hị́ ọ́   'he called him'
ộ hụ́ ọ́   'he boiled it'

(See §3.1 for juncture prosodies with regard to close vowels.)

High tone is a marker of the object pronominal piece common to all the examples of harmony span in the VP given above.

The preverbs, represented by *o/ọ* in the above examples, may be up to three sequences of vowels carrying complex tones which denote various grammatical features. Even in such cases, the harmony span of the VP is never broken. (See chapter 4 for full description of the preverbs.)

Harmony in the verb word. The vowel sequences in verbal lexical words of CVCV pattern are limited to vowels within each set.

Set A: *i, e, o, u, a* in CVCV verb words

i-i	zìzí	'to shake'
i-e	círê	'to wear clothes'
i-o	–	–
i-u	–	–
i-a	zìnà	'to roll'

e-i	téɲí	'to repair'
e-e	pèhè	'to winnow'
e-o	–	–
e-u	–	–
e-a	cémâ	'to lift up'

o-i	–	–
o-e	–	–
o-o	vòvó	'to put a child on the back'
o-u	–	–
o-a	zózà	'to be beautiful'

u-i	–	–
u-e	rúré	'to be tough'
u-o	–	–
u-u	kùrú	'to tie a knot'
u-a	tùrà	'to pull'

a-i	dàhí	'to be well'
a-e	–	–
a-o	–	–
a-u	vàgù	'to forgive'
a-a	hàrà	'to gather'

Set B: *i̱, e̱, o̱, u̱, a* in CVCV verb words

i̱-i̱	pi̱rí̱	'to squeeze with force'
i̱-e̱	cí̱ne̱	'to prepare/boil meat'
i̱-o̱	–	–
i̱-u̱	–	–
i̱-a	ɲi̱ná	'to wash'

e̱-i̱	ge̱rí̱	'to meet'
e̱-e̱	ce̱rè̱	'to write'
e̱-o̱	–	–
e̱-u̱	–	–
e̱-a	ne̱ba	'to be high'

Phonology

ọ-ị	–	–
ọ-ẹ	–	–
ọ-ọ	hòkó̩	'to rinse'
ọ-u	–	–
ọ-a	hó̩há	'to be greedy'
ụ-ị	–	–
ụ-e	múnẹ	'to swallow'
ụ-o	–	–
ụ-ụ	sụ̀tụ́	'to lie dead'
ụ-a	tụrâ	'to build'
a-ị	bànị́	'to sift flour'
a-ẹ	–	–
a-ọ	–	–
a-u	dàgù	'to smell'
a-a	wara	'to fry'

The tables below give the summary of sets A and B CVCV pattern cooccurrence restrictions.

Set A

2ND VOWEL

	i	e	o	u	a
i	x	x			x
e	x	x			x
o			x		x
u	x	x			x
a	x			x	x

1ST VOWEL

Set B

2ND VOWEL

	ị	ẹ	ọ	ụ	a
ị	x	x			x
ẹ	x	x			x
ọ			x		x
ụ	x	x			x
a	x			x	x

1ST VOWEL

For two-syllable verbs, the second vowel is usually identical with the first vowel. The close vowels can also take the half-close vowels in the second syllable. Only /a/ can cooccur in any combination with any other vowel of either set.

Comment on /a/. /a/ has occurrence restrictions with vowel set A. Words have not been found in the language with the sequence *o-a* and *u-a* in VCV pattern.

The fact that /a/ has no cooccurrence restrictions with vowel set B might suggest that /a/ belonged to vowel set B originally and in the course of time has extended its function to vowel set A. Another possibility is that vowel set A had a counterpart of /a/ originally (in proto Ebira, probably [ə] or [ʌ]) but the phonetic distinction between this vowel and [a] was lost and /a/ now additionally carries the functional load of the missing vowel. Speculative phonology is not part of the focus of this thesis. This comment is just a suggestion as to why there are some cooccurrence restrictions with vowel set A and there are none with vowel set B.

The discussion of Ebira vowel harmony systems is by no means exhaustive here. But the examples given here do highlight the important role of this phenomenon in the phonology and grammar of the language. Detailed description of the preverbs in their harmonic sets within the verbal piece is given in chapter 4. Furthermore, harmony principles are illustrated in Ebira sentence examples given in all the sections of this thesis. Instrumental recording of some harmonic pairs is presented in Appendix 3.

The adverbs and ideophones. The lexical verbal class includes adverbs and ideophones. Although the term adverb is applied to some lexical items in Ebira, these adverbs differ in function and syntactic order from adverbs in English. Examine the following English sentences and their Ebira equivalents.

ENGLISH   EBIRA

(a) He speaks **loudly**   *ọ̀ kàréyi tụ́ ẹ̀ba*
                      he speak put up

(b) He speaks **strongly**   *ọ̀ sị́ ọŋwẹ ọ́kátẹ́ŋụ́ karẹ́yi*
                      he take voice strong speak

(c) He speaks **quickly**   *ọ̀ sị́ eyíhá kárẹ́yi*
                      he take haste speak

(d) He speaks **gently**   *ọ̀ tàŋwà kàréyi*
                      he gently speaks

Phonology

In the English sentences above all the words in bold face type are adverbs and all these adverbs occur sentence final, although some of the adverbs could occur preceding the verb in some styles of English. In Ebira there is no adverb at all in sentences (a) – (c). The function of the adverb is carried by serial verbs and nominal phrases in these sentences. It is only in sentence (d) of Ebira that there is an adverb *tàŋwà*, 'gently', and it precedes the verb.

There are very few PURE adverbs in Ebira. These adverbs fall into two classes, those which occur preceding the verb and those which occur following the verb. The words in bold face type are adverbs in the following examples.

nâ búrú
go quickly
'go quickly'

jĕ gérí
stand firmly
'stand firmly'

tàŋwà kàréyi
gently speak
'speak gently'

wùsè rísa
quickly eat
'eat quickly'

Adverbs can be reduplicated for intensity in whatever position they occur, either before or after the verb.

Adverbs and ideophones are very similar in structure and function. Ideophones are items which add particular intensity and sound effect to a sentence in Ebira. Reduplication is a feature of ideophones.

Ideophones always occur after the verbs, e.g.:

izèɲì ộ súreyi woroɲi-woroɲi
bell it sound
'the bell sounded *"woronyi-woronyi"*'

uṇọ́kọ ộ chàká núgù-nùgù
pot it break
'the pot broke *"núgù-nùgù"*'

A few more ideophones are listed below:

bemi-bemi	CVCV-CVCV	'wholly, completely'
zịnâ-zịnâ	CVCV̂-CVCV̂	'forever and ever, eternally'
sẹnẹ-sẹnẹ	CVCV-CVCV	
sẹẹsẹnẹ	CVVCVCV	'very, very white'

sákásáká	CV́CV́-CV́CV́	⎫
sáásáká	CV́V́CV́CV́	⎬ 'completely, all'
vànà-vànà	CV̀CV̀-CV̀CV̀	⎫ 'to be very uncomfortable
vààvànà	CV̀V̀CV̀CV̀	⎬ in sickness or pain'
vànàà	CV̀CV̀V̀	⎭
bonoko-bonoko	CVCVCV-CVCVCV	⎫ 'to be big
bonokoo	CVCVCVV	⎬ and shapeless'

Reduplication processes manifest some interesting phonological changes including metathesis. We need not give any emphasis to these here. It is worth noting, however, that the development of geminate vowel sequences medially and finally, mentioned in §2.2, can be observed from the alternate forms of the reduplicated words above.

2.4 Syllabic Nasals

As mentioned in §2.1, syllable type 2 consists of a syllabic nasal plus tone and is followed immediately in the word by a CV syllable. The syllabic nasal may occur in words of either vowel harmony set A or B and does not interrupt the harmonic sequence system of the vowels. The syllabic nasal is always homorganic in point of articulation with the following consonant.

Bilabial syllabic nasal

/m/ [m] voiced bilabial syllabic nasal preceding bilabial consonants.

m-p	àm̀pò	'a bag'
m-b	ịhím̀ba	'seven'
m-m	ḿ màá vẹ̀	'when I was coming . . . '

Alveolar syllabic nasal

/n/ [n] voiced alveolar syllabic nasal preceding alveolar consonants.

n-t	ọ̀ǹtẹ̀	'a typewriter'
n-d	ǹdá	'father'
n-n	ịhíńnà	'nine'

Phonology

Palatal syllabic nasal

/ɲ/ [ɲ] voiced palatal syllabic nasal preceding palatal and affricate consonants.

ɲ-ɲ	ɲ̀ɲá	'mother'
ɲ-c	ò̩ɲcé̩rè̩	'monkey'
ɲ-j	è̩jaɲ́jako	'dotted maize cob'

Velar syllabic nasal

/ŋ/ /ŋ/ voiced velar nasal preceding velar consonants.

| ŋ-k | ì̩kò̩ŋ́kò̩ | 'bathing sponge' |
| ŋ-g | aŋ́go̩ | 'yam seedling' |

Summary of syllabic nasals

/m/ precedes /p/, /b/ and /m/.
/n/ precedes /t/, /d/ and /n/.
/ɲ/ precedes /ɲ/, /c/ and /j/.
/ŋ/ precedes /k/ and /g/.

A syllabic nasal is always followed by a homorganic stop, affricate, or an identical nasal.

The other consonants in the language are not preceded by syllabic nasals.

2.5 The Consonant Phonemes

Ebira has nineteen consonant phonemes.

Description

All the consonants are made with egressive lung air:

/p/ [pʰ]   voiceless bilabial slightly aspirated plosive
               /pà/   [pʰà]   'to beg'

/b/ [b]   voiced bilabial plosive
               /bà/   [bà]   'to dig'

/t/ [tʰ]   voiceless alveolar slightly aspirated plosive
               /tá/   [tʰá]   'to weave (a rope)'

/d/ [d]   voiced alveolar plosive
               /dà/   [dà]   'to cut'

/k/ [kʰ]   voiceless velar slightly aspirated plosive
             /kà/   [kʰà]   'to tell, to say'

/g/ [g]   voiced velar plosive
             /gà/   [gà]   'to divide'

All the voiceless plosives are slightly aspirated but this is not distinctive, and will not be indicated in the transcription from now on.

/v/ [v]   voiced labiodental fricative
             /vé̩/   [vé̩]   'to come'

/s/ [s]   voiceless alveolar grooved fricative
             /sí̩/   [sí̩]   'to take'

    [ʃ]   voiceless alveopalatal grooved fricative
             [ʃ] is an allophone of /s/ across morpheme boundaries in certain phonological conditions. This will be described later.

/z/ [z]   voiced alveolar grooved fricative
             /zì/   [zì]   'to filter'

    [ʒ]   voiced alveopalatal grooved fricative
             [ʒ] is an allophone of /z/ across morpheme boundaries in certain phonological conditions. It will be described along with [ʃ].

/h/ [h]   voiceless glottal fricative
             /hí̩/   [hí̩]   'to call'

/c/ [c]   voiceless alveopalatal affricate.
             /cí̩/   [cí̩]   'to get nuts out of the
                                        shell with fingers'

/j/ [j]   voiced alveopalatal affricate
             /ji/   [ji]   'to cut stick with hand'

/m/ [m]   voiced bilabial nasal
             /mè̩/   [mè̩]   'to do, to make'

/n/ [n]   voiced alveolar nasal
             /ne/   [ne]   'to throw'

/ɲ/	[ɲ]	voiced palatal nasal			
		/ɲá/	[ɲá]		'to hit'
/ŋ/	[ŋ]	voiced velar nasal			
		/ŋu̞/	[ŋu̞]		'to enter'
/r/	[r]	voiced alveolar tap			
		/rí/	[lí]		'to eat'
	[l]	voiced alveolar lateral			
		[l] is in free variation with /r/ but most people use /r/ in their speech.			
/w/	[w]	voiced bilabial semivowel			
		/wu̞/	[wu̞]		'to kill'
/y/	[y]	voiced palatal semivowel			
		/yé̞/	[yé̞]		'to know'

Consonant allophones and conditioning

[ʃ] and [ʒ]. [ʃ] and [ʒ] occur as allophones of /s/ and /z/ respectively under the following phonological conditions:

/s/ in the sequence [sí] followed by a nonclose vowel initial syllable across morpheme boundaries is realized as [ʃ]. The sounds in focus are indicated by boldface type in the following examples:

STRUCTURE: VP + NP₀

si̞	+	e:	ô	si̞	+	ècè	vé̞	>	ôʃècè vé̞
			he	took		wine	came		'he brought some wine'

si̞	+	e̞:	ô	si̞	+	e̞za	vé̞	>	ôʃé̞za vé̞
			he	took		beans	came		'he brought some beans'

si	+	o:	ô	si̞	+	ozí	vé̞	>	ôʃózí vé̞
			he	took		child	came		'he brought the child'

si̞	+	o̞:	ô	si̞	+	o̞cí	vé̞	>	ôʃó̞cí vé̞
			he	took		stick	came		'he brought the stick'

si̞	+	a:	ô	si̞	+	aje̞	vé̞	>	ôʃáje̞ vé̞
			he	took		egg	came		'he brought the eggs'

Similarly /z/ in the sequence [zi] followed by a nonclose vowel initial syllable is realized as [ʒ].

STRUCTURE: VP + NP$_O$
            [zi] 'to hurt' + NP$_O$

zị	+	e:	ộ zị	+	ezí	> ộ ʒezí
			it hurt		children	'it hurt the children'
zị	+	ẹ:	ộ zị	+	eŋú	> ộ ʒeŋú
			it hurt		body	'it hurt the body, i.e. he felt the pain'
zị	+	o:	ộ zị	+	ozí	> ộ ʒozí
			it hurt		child	'it hurt the child'
zị	+	ọ:	ộ zị	+	ọ̀zà	> ộ ʒọ̀zà
			it hurt		person	'it hurt a person'
zị	+	a:	ộ zị	+	àzà	> ộ ʒàzà
			it hurt		people	'it hurt the people'

On the other hand, /s/ and /z/ retain their phonetic qualities in sequence [si] or [zi] followed by close vowels.

sị	+	i:	ộ sị	+	ìzì vẹ́	> ộ sízí vẹ́
			he took		nuts came	'he brought bambara nuts'
sị	+	ị:	ộ sị	+	ịŋò vẹ́	> ộ síŋò vẹ́
			he took		scales came	'he brought the scales'
sị	+	u:	ộ sị	+	uye vẹ́	> ộ súye vẹ́
			he took		meat came	'he brought some meat'
sị	+	ụ:	ộ sị	+	ùrá vẹ́	> ộ súrá vẹ́
			he took		pig came	'he brought a pig'
zị	+	i:	ộ zị	+	ìzé	> ộ zìzé
			it hurt		ize	'it hurt Ize'
zị	+	ị:	ộ zị	+	ịcà	> ộ zịcà
			it hurt		ica	'it hurt Ica'
zị	+	u:	ộ zị	+	ùrú	> ộ zùrú
			it hurt		ùrú	'it hurt Uru'

Phonology

zị + ụ: ọ̀ zị + ụ̀nọ   >   ọ̀ zụ̀nọ
        it hurt   cow   'it hurt the cow'

Chart of the consonant phonemes

The following chart gives a graphic display of Ebira consonants.

		Labial	Alveolar	Palatal	Velar	Glottal
Plosives	vls	p	t		k	
	vd	b	d		g	
Fricatives	vls		s			h
	vd	v	z			
Affricates	vls			c		
	vd			j		
Nasals	vls					
	vd	m	n	ɲ	ŋ	
Laterals	vls					
	vd		r			
Semivowels	vls					
	vd	w		y		

All the consonants can occur as syllable margin in word initial and word medial positions but never syllable or word final.

Note that the consonantal features, labialization and palatalization, are described in §2.1.

Throughout this work, the palatal and velar nasals are written phonemically as $ɲ$ and $ŋ$. In the practical orthography for the language, however, they are written as *ny* and *ng* respectively.

2.6 Tone

Tone in Ebira functions at two distinct levels: the lexical level and the grammatical level.

Tone symbolization

Tone is symbolized as follows:

High tone	H	marked	´
Mid tone	M	unmarked	
Low tone	L	marked	`
High-Falling tone	HF	marked	ˆ
Low-Rising tone	LR	marked	ˇ
Down Step	H'	marked	'

Automatic tone downstep occurs only under specific tone contractions of HLH → H'H (see §3.4).

It can be observed from the above that Ebira has three level tones and two kinetic tones. Lexical tone is directly related to the syllable structure as stated in §2.1. Every syllable has a tonal feature as one of its phonological components.

Tone distribution

The level tones (high, mid, and low) have a very wide distribution. The two kinetic tones (high-falling and low-rising) do not occur word initial or word medial, except high-falling tone which occurs on the one syllable verb prefix denoting person and number. The low-rising tone [ˇ] is found to occur only in the nine monosyllabic verbs listed below:

hě   'to be in possession of something by finding it'
rě   'to lick (some liquid soup or oil)'
ɲě   'to wipe (with hand, cloth, or duster)'
jě   'to stand, to wait'
zě   'to answer'
rǒ   'to make a hole through a wall or a door'
nǒ   'to make public announcement with special gong'
tǒ   'to pick up small items from the ground'
ɲǎ   'to break palm kernels with stones to get the seeds out'

Lexical tone on monosyllabic verbs

At the lexical level, tone is phonemic in that it minimally distinguishes two or more lexical items. It is easy to observe some lexical contrasts on

Phonology

monosyllabic items especially verbs of CV syllable structure. Tone is an identificational feature of the verb word.

Sets of two contrastive tone verbs:

High	sí	'to pay'
Low	sì	'to look for, to want'
High	ɲí	'to have'
Mid	ɲi̩	'to choose'
Low	hò̩	'to ask'
Mid	ho̩	'to drive'
High	hé	'to excrete body waste (urine and feces)'
Low-Rising	hě	'to be in possession of something by finding it'
Mid	no̩	'to weave (a mat)'
Low-Rising	nǒ̩	'to make public announcement with special gong'
Low	rò	'to think'
Low-Rising	rǒ	'to make a hole through a wall or a door'
High	jé̩	'to be happy'
Low-Rising	jě̩	'to wait'
High	yí	'to steal'
High-Falling	yî	'to refuse'

Sets of three contrastive tone verbs:

High	hú	'to drink'
Mid	hu	'to uproot'
Low	hù	'to roast in open fire'
High	tó̩	'to chew'
Low	tò̩	'to prepare mud for building walls of a house'
Low-Rising	tǒ̩	'to pick little items from the floor'

Sets of four contrastive tone verbs are extremely rare. The only set found so far is listed below:

High	ná	'to sell'
Mid	na	'to open'
Low	nà	'to tear'
High-Falling	nâ	'to leave'

Sets of five contrastive tone words have not been found in the language.

A table of monosyllabic verbs that contrast solely in lexical tone is given in appendix A.

Lexical tone patterns on disyllabic verbs

A full range of nine lexical tone patterns that can occur on two CVCV syllable verbs are exemplified below:

1. HH [⁻ ⁻]   hárá   'to plane (wood)'
2. HM [⁻ ⁻]   dúdu   'to be together in action'
3. HL [⁻ _]   hínè   'to be sweet'
4. MH [⁻ ⁻]   diví   'to be bad'
5. MM [⁻ ⁻]   hara   'to scratch lightly'
6. ML [⁻ _]   tẹsì   'to care for'
7. LH [_ ⁻]   hèɲí   'to shake'
8. LM [_ ⁻]   vìdị   'to be first'
9. LL [_ _]   hàrà   'to gather'

Verbs of more than two syllables have extended pattern using the same high, mid, and low tones.

Lexical tone on disyllabic nouns

Tone also distinguishes two or more nominal lexical items of VCV syllable structure.

Sets of two contrastive tone nouns:

usé   'cough'
ùsè   'question'

ihì   'a case (usually long); fossils'
ihî   'loss'

aɲá   'blood'
áɲa   'dew'

Sets of three contrastive tone nouns:

urú   'a kind of native red ointment worn by women who just delivered a new baby'
ùrú   'replacement of something on demand, compensation'
ùrù   'mushroom'

Phonology

o̩da	'a native tray'
ò̩dà	'paint, tarmac'
ó̩dâ	'law, order, command'

Sets of four contrastive tone nouns are rare but they do occur:

ohi	'broom'
ohí	'whistle'
òhí	'a leader'
òhì	'answer'

Lexical tone patterns on disyllabic nouns

A system of eleven contrastive tone patterns occurs on two VCV syllable nouns.

1.	HH	[‾ ‾]	i̩dá	'a place'
2.	HM	[‾ —]	íze	'a grass cutter (animal)'
3.	HL	[‾ _]	ákù	'inner room'
4.	MH	[— ‾]	ahẹ́	'song'
5.	MM	[— —]	uye	'meat'
6.	ML	[— _]	anè	'egret'
7.	LH	[_ ‾]	òsé	'wife'
8.	LM	[_ —]	òru	'crow'
9.	LL	[_ _]	i̩dù	'lion'
10.	HHF	[‾ ⌐]	ó̩dâ	'law'
11.	MHF	[— ⌐]	ihî	'loss'

Nouns of more than three syllables have an extended pattern, using the same high, mid, and low tones.

These nouns and verbs are described here in relation to tones in isolation only. Examples of tone changes which occur when they function in the verbal piece are discussed in later chapters.

3 Syntactic Junctures

The major syntactic juncture features of Ebira concern vowel elision, tone changes, and syllable prosodies. Each of these features is described within the grammatical structure of Ebira sentences.

3.1 Vowel Elision

As Ebira is an open-syllable language, the last segment of any word is always a vowel. The first segment of nominals, with the possible exception of certain bound pronouns, is always a vowel, while verbals and some function words always start with consonants. Therefore, very frequently two vowels, labelled here as V_1 and V_2, come into juxtaposition. V_1 is the final vowel of the first item, and V_2 is the initial vowel of the second item. Within a grammatical phrase one of the two juxtaposed vowels is elided and the other one is retained. (The only condition in which both vowels are retained is described in §3.4.)

The nine vowel phonemes of the language can be divided into two classes according to their functional manifestations at boundary junctures. These are close vowels and nonclose vowels. The diagram below shows the divisions and their phonematic unit representations. The phonematic units are enclosed in parentheses.

			FRONT	CENTRAL	BACK
1	CLOSE	Raised	i (I)		u (U)
		Lowered	$i̥$		$u̥$
2	NONCLOSE	Raised	e (E)		o (O)
		Lowered	$e̥$	a (A)	$o̥$

In a simple grammatical VP + NP$_0$ structure the following pattern of vowel elisions occur:

Close vowels *i* and *u* as V$_1$ and V$_2$

In the following examples the close vowels *i, i̧, u,* and *u̧* are presented in words and sentences to illustrate the pattern of elision that takes place when they occur in V$_1$ position and in V$_2$ position contiguously in certain grammatical structures.

I **as V1 and as V2.** The monosyllabic verb of CV structure /sì/ 'to want', is used as a typical word where the final vowel is /i/, that is V$_1$. Similarly, the verb /sí̧/ 'to take', is used as a typical word having /i̧/ as its final vowel, V$_1$. Nominals having /i/ and /i̧/ as their initial vowels, such as in /ìzì/ 'bambara nuts' and /i̧ŋɔ̀/ 'scales', illustrate /i/ and /i̧/ as V$_2$ at word junctures. When the vowels /i/ and /i̧/ are juxtaposed at word junctions, in either order, /i̧/ is elided and /i/ is retained. That means that the raised close front vowel /i/ dominates the lowered close front vowel /i̧/ at word junctions. Tones are marked in the examples that follow as there is tone movement or tone replacement when a vowel is elided. Tone movement is described in §3.4.

i	+	*i*	>	*i*	sì + ìzì	>	sìzì
					want bambara nuts		
					ô sìzì	'He wanted bambara nuts.'	
i	+	*i̧*	>	*i*	sì + i̧ŋɔ̀	>	sìŋɔ̀
					want scale		
					ô sìŋɔ̀	'He wanted the scales.'	
i̧	+	*i*	>	*i*	sí̧ + ìzì	>	sízì
					take bambara nuts		
					ô sízì	'He took bambara nuts.'	
i̧	+	*i̧*	>	*i̧*	sí̧ + i̧ŋɔ̀	>	sí̧ŋɔ̀
					take scale		
					ô sí̧ŋɔ̀	'He took the scales.'	

I **as V$_1$; *U* as V$_2$.** The verbs /sì/ and /sí̧/ (see §3.1) are used here again as words having final /i/ and final /i̧/. The nominals /ùjì/ 'basket' and /u̧jì/ 'sugar cane' are used as examples of typical words having /u/ and /u̧/ as initial vowels. When /i/ occurs as V$_1$ and /u/ as V$_2$, /i/ is elided and /u/ is retained. When /i/ occurs as V$_1$ and /u̧/ occurs as V$_2$, neither is retained; instead the resulting vowel is /u/. When /i̧/ occurs as V$_1$ and /u/ occurs as

Syntactic Junctures 47

V₂, /i̯/ is elided and /u/ is retained. The following examples illustrate these changes.

i	+	u	>	u	sì + ùjì > sùjì
					look for basket
					ô sùjì 'He looked for the basket'

i	+	u̩	>	u	sì + u̩ji̩ > suji̩
					look for sugar cane
					ô suji̩ 'He looked for the sugar cane.'

i̩	+	u	>	u	sí + ùjì > sújì
					take basket
					ọ́ sújì 'He took the basket.'

i̩	+	u̩	>	u̩	sí + u̩ji̩ > súji̩
					take sugar cane
					ọ́ súji̩ 'He took the sugar cane.'

In summary, every vowel has two qualities out of the four given:

1. Raised or lowered;
2. Front or back.

In every combination of two close vowels (one final in a word and the other initial in the following word) in a phrase, the resulting vowel is raised excluding lowered and back excluding front.

The same elision rules apply whatever the nature of the consonant that precedes V₁.

All the preceding examples illustrate the grammatical sequence VP + NP. The same pattern of elision takes place within all grammatical phrases. Examples illustrate the same combinations in the structure:

```
(N    +    N)   +   VP
      NP        +   VP
```

The junction of NP + VP will be commented on later.

i	+	i	>	i	ozí + izé + ọ vẹ́
					child Ize he came
					N + N VP
					NP + VP
					ozízé ọ vẹ́
					'Ize's child came.'

i + *i̱* > *i*   ozí + i̱cà + ǫ̂ vę́
                child   Ica   he came
                N   +   N   VP
                    NP   +   VP
              ozícà   *ǫ̂ vę́*
              'Ica's child came.'

i + *u* > *u*   ozí + ùrú + ǫ̂ nâ
                child   Uru   he go
                N   +   N   VP
                    NP   +   VP
              ozùrú   *ǫ̂ nâ*
              'Uru's child went.'

i + *u̱* > *u*   ozí + umu̱sá + ǫ̂ nâ
                child   Umusa   he go
                N   +   N   VP
                    NP   +   VP
              ozúmu̱sá   *ǫ̂ nâ*
              'Umusa's child went.'

In this structure there is usually a pause between the NP functioning as subject and the VP, therefore no elision takes place at this juncture. But it is also possible to pronounce the clause in rapid speech without a pause between the NP and the VP, in which case the rules for elision being described would operate.

U as V_1; *I* as V_2. The verbs /tú/ 'to beat' and /du̱/ 'to chase' are used here as typical words having /u/ and /u̱/ as final vowels. The nominals /izé/ 'Ize, feminine name' and /i̱cà/ 'masculine name' are used as words having /i/ and /i̱/ as their initial vowels. When /u/ occurs as V_1 and /i/ occurs as V_2, /i/ is elided and /u/ is retained. When /u/ occurs as V_1 and /i̱/ occurs as V_2, /i̱/ is elided and /u/ is retained. When /u̱/ occurs as V_1 and /i/ occurs as V_2, /u/ is the resulting vowel. When /u̱/ occurs as V_1 and /i̱/ as V_2, /i̱/ is elided and /u̱/ is retained. These changes are illustrated in the following examples:

u + *i* > *u*   *tú*   +   *ìzé* > *túzé*
                beat   Ize
                                ô   *túzé*
                                'He beat Ize.'

Syntactic Junctures

u + i̩ > u tú + i̩cà > túcà
                beat   Ica
                           ô túcà
                           'He beat Ica.'

u̩ + i > u du̩ + izé > duzé
                chase   Ize
                            ô duzé
                            'He chased Ize.'

u̩ + i̩ > u̩ du̩ + i̩cà > du̩cà
                 chase   Ica
                            ô du̩cà
                           'He chased Ica.'

The consonants (*t-* and *d-*) here, segments of the syllables and/or words, are typical of other consonants when they occur in combination with /U/ to form words. Whatever consonant precedes /U/, the pattern of elision would be the same as the one described in §3.1 above.

In the (N + N)NP structure where *U* is V_1 and I or *U* occur as V_2 the pattern of elision is identical with that of VP + NP (see §2.1). The following two examples are given for further illustration.

u + i > u   uvú + izé + ô diví
                madness Ize   it bad
                N   + N   + VP
                uvúzé ô divi
                'Ize's madness is bad/serious.'

u + u̩ > u   uvú + u̩músá + ô tá
                madness Umusa it finish
                N   + N   + VP
                Uvumu̩sa ô tá
                'Umusa's madness is finished,' i.e.
                'Umusa is healed of madness.'

Here again, because there is a natural pause between the NP functioning as the subject and the VP in the above structure, no elision takes place between the NP final vowel and the VP initial vowel, even though the two vowels come into juxtaposition.

U as V_1 and as V_2. The verbs /tú/ 'to beat/hit' and /du̩/ 'to chase' are used as examples of typical words which show the pattern of elision. When /u/ occurs as V_1; and /u̩/ occurs as V_2, V_2 is elided and V_1 is retained, that is, /u/ is retained. When /ụ/ occurs as V_1 and /u/ as V_2, then V_2, /u/, is retained.

The nominals /usú/ 'rat' and /ụvá/ 'crocodile' are used to illustrate words having /u/ and /ụ/ as the initial vowels.

$u + u > u$ tú + usú > túsú
                hit   rat
                ô túsú
                'He hit a rat.'

$u + ụ > u$ tú + ụvá > túvá
                hit   crocodile
                ô túvá
                'He hit a crocodile.'

$ụ + u > u$ dụ + usú > dụsú
                chase rat
                ô dụsú
                'He chased a rat.'

$ụ + ụ > ụ$ dụ + ụvá > dụvá
                chase crocodile
                ô dụvá
                'He chased a crocodile.'

It is evident from these examples that the raised close back vowel /u/ dominates the raised and lowered close front vowels /i/ and /ị/, and the lowered close back vowel /ụ/ at word junctions.

Close vowels as V_1, nonclose vowels as V_2. The pattern of elision is illustrated below.

I **as V_1; and the nonclose vowels, *e*, *o* and *a* as V_2.** When either of the close front vowels, /i/ or /ị/, come into juxtaposition with any of the nonclose vowels, *e*, *ẹ*, *o*, *ọ*, and a at word junctions, the close vowel is elided and the nonclose vowel is retained.

Two verbs, /yí/ 'to steal' and /jị/ 'to cut' are used in sentences of VP + NP structure to illustrate the elision pattern of close front vowel in V_1 position.

$i + e > e$ yí + ècé > yécè
                steal wine
                ô yécè hú
                'He stole some wine and drank it.'

Syntactic Junctures

i	+	ẹ	>	ẹ	yí + ẹ̀bà	> yẹ́bà	
					steal chain		
					ô yẹ́bà		
					'He stole the chain.'		
ị	+	ẹ	>	ẹ	jị + ẹ̀bà	> jẹ̀bà	
					cut chain		
					ô jẹ̀bà		
					'He cut the chain off the door.'		

Similarly:

i	+	o	>	o	yí	+	òbó >	yóbó	'steal a rope'
i	+	ọ	>	ọ	yí	+	ọcị́ >	yọ́cị́	'steal a cane'
i	+	a	>	a	yí	+	àgá >	yágá	'steal a chair'
ị	+	e	>	e	jị	+	ègú >	jègú	'cut small tribal marks'
ị	+	o	>	o	jị	+	òbó >	jòbó	'cut a rope'
ị	+	ọ	>	ọ	jị	+	ọcị́ >	jọcị́	'cut a stick'
ị	+	a	>	a	jị	+	avị́ >	javị́	'cut a leaf'

For a description of syllable prosodies that occur when the consonant preceding *I* is *s, z,* or *h,* see §3.3. For all other consonants the elision pattern is as illustrated above.

U as V₁; and the nonclose vowels e, o, a as V₂. The close back vowels, /u/ and /ụ/ in V_1 position and nonclose vowels listed above in V_2 position at word junctions give rise to labial syllable prosody. This is described in detail in §3.2. However, two examples are given here to illustrate phonetic characteristics of the vowels in juxtaposition.

tu	+	e	>	^we	tú + ezí	> $t^wézí$	'beat the children'
					ô $t^wézí$	ené yí èkẹ̀hị̀	
					he beat children	who stole money	
					'He beat the children who stole the money.'		
dụ	+	ẹ	>	$d^wẹ$	dụ + evụ́	> $d^wevụ́$	'chase a goat'
					ô $d^wevụ$	kánâ	
					he chase goat	away	
					'He chased the goat away.'		

Nonclose vowels e, o, a as V₁

When a nonclose vowel occurs in V_1 position, there is regularity in the pattern of elision. V_1 is always elided and V_2 retained. It does not matter which vowel occurs in V_2 position, whether it is a close vowel or a nonclose vowel. In the next examples, using again the VP + NP structure, the pattern of elision is illustrated.

It will be noticed that the preverb /o/ or /ọ/ retains in the elided forms of the phrase the quality which it has in the nonelided forms. On the surface, this appears to violate the rules of vowel harmony, but in fact the preverb maintains the harmony it has with its verb, and this helps to preserve and identify this verb semantically.

e as V₁

(a) *e* as V₁ in VP /ré/ 'to see' + V₂

e	+	i	>	i	ré	+	ìsì	>	rísì
					ô rísì				'He saw a fly.'
e	+	ị	>	ị	ré	+	ịta	>	rítà
					ô rítà				'He saw the cloth.'
e	+	u	>	u	ré	+	uné	>	rúne
					ô rúné				'He saw a gazelle.'
e	+	ụ	>	ụ	ré	+	ùnọ	>	rúnọ
					ô rúnọ				'He saw a cow.'
e	+	e	>	e	ré	+	ekú	'>	rékú
					ô rékú				'He saw a masquerade.'
e	+	ẹ	>	ẹ	ré	+	evú	>	rẹ́vú
					ô rẹ́vú				'He saw a goat.'
e	+	o	>	o	ré	+	ozí	>	rózí
					ô rózí				'He saw a child.'
e	+	ọ	>	ọ	ré	+	òzà	>	rọ̀zà
					ô rọ́zà				'He saw a person.'
e	+	a	>	a	ré	+	àzà	>	rázà
					ô rázà				'He saw some people.'

(b) *ẹ* as V₁ in VP /mè/ 'to make' + V₂

ẹ	+	i	>	i	mè	+	ìhì	>	mìhì
					ộ mìhì				'He made a quiver.'
ẹ	+	ị	>	ị	mè	+	ịsá	>	mịsá
					ộ mịsá				'He cooked food.'
ẹ	+	u	>	u	mè	+	ùjì	>	mùjì
					ộ mùjì				'He made a basket.'
ẹ	+	ụ	>	ụ	mè	+	ùhú	>	mùhú
					ộ mùhú				'He made a brush.'
ẹ	+	e	>	e	mè	+	ècè	>	mècè
					ộ mècè				'He made wine.'
ẹ	+	ẹ	>	ẹ	mè	+	ẹ̀kọ́	>	mẹ̀kọ́
					ộ mẹ̀kọ́				'He cooked porridge.'

Syntactic Junctures

ẹ	+	o	>	o	mẹ̀ + óre	>	móre	
					ô móre			'He cooked water yam cake.'
ẹ	+	ọ	>	ọ	mẹ̀ + ọ̀kụ́	>	mọ̀kụ́	
					ô mọ̀kụ́			'He made a sickle.'
ẹ	+	a	>	a	mẹ̀ + àgá	>	màgá	
					ô màgá			'He made a chair.'

o as V₁

(a) *o* as V₁ in VP /tò/ 'to arrange' + V₂

o	+	i	>	i	tò + ìhì	>	tìhì	
					ô tìhì			'He arranged the quivers.'
o	+	ị	>	ị	tò + ịtà	>	tịtà	
					ô tịtà			'He arranged the pieces of cloth.'
o	+	u	>	u	tò + ùjì	>	tùjì	
					ô tùjì			'He arranged the baskets.'
o	+	ụ	>	ụ	tò + ụjị	>	tụjị	
					ô tụjị			'He arranged the sugar canes.'
o	+	e	>	e	tò + ezí	>	tezí	
					ô tezí			'He arranged the children.'
o	+	ẹ	>	ẹ	tò + ẹɲá	>	tẹɲá	
					ô tẹɲá			'He arranged the loads.'
o	+	o	>	o	tò + òbó	>	tòbó	
					ô tòbó			'He arranged the ropes.'
o	+	ọ	>	ọ	tò + ọhá	>	tọhá	
					ô tọhá			'He arranged the spears.'
o	+	a	>	a	tò + àzà	>	tàzà	
					ô tàzà			'He arranged the people.'

(b) *ọ* as V₁ in VP /dọ́/ 'to get' + V₂

ọ	+	i	>	i	dọ́ + ìhì	>	dìhì	
					ô díhì			'He got the quiver.'
ọ	+	ị	>	ị	dọ́ + ịtà	>	dítà	
					ô dítà			'He got the cloth.'
ọ	+	u	>	u	dọ́ + ùjì	>	dújì	
					ô dújì			'He got the basket.'
ọ	+	ụ	>	ụ	dọ́ + ụjị	>	dújị	
					ô dújị			'He got the sugar cane.'
ọ	+	e	>	e	dọ́ + ezí	>	dézí	
					ô dézí			'He got the children.'
ọ	+	ẹ	>	ẹ	dọ́ + ẹɲá	>	déɲá	
					ô déɲá			'He got the load.'
ọ	+	o	>	o	dọ́ + ozí	>	dózí	
					ô dózí			'He got the child.'

ọ	+	ọ	>	ọ	dọ́	+	ọhá	>	dọ́há
					ọ̀ dọ́há				'He got a spear.'
ọ	+	a	>	a	dọ́	+	àzà	>	dázà
					ọ̀ dázà				'He got the people.'

a as V₁. *a* as V₁ in VP /ná/ 'to sell' + V₂

a	+	i	>	i	ná	+	ihì	>	níhì
					ọ̀ níhì				'He sold a quiver.'
a	+	ị	>	ị	ná	+	ịtà	>	nị́tà
					ọ̀ nị́tà				'He sold cloth.'
a	+	u	>	u	ná	+	uye	>	núye
					ọ̀ nuye				'He sold meat.'
a	+	ụ	>	ụ	ná	+	ụ̀rá	>	nụ́rá
					ọ̀ nụ́rá				'He sold a pig.'
a	+	e	>	e	ná	+	ècè	>	nécè
					ọ̀ nécè				'He sold wine.'
a	+	ẹ	>	ẹ	ná	+	ẹzẹ́	>	nẹ́zẹ́
					ọ̀ nẹ́zẹ́				'He sold a big drum.'
a	+	o	>	o	ná	+	òbó	>	nóbó
					ọ̀ nóbó				'He sold a rope.'
a	+	ọ	>	ọ	ná	+	ọhá	>	nọ́há
					ọ̀ nọ́há				'He sold a spear.'
a	+	a	>	a	ná	+	àgá	>	nágá
					ọ̀ nágá				'He sold a chair.'

Summary chart of vowel elision patterns

The following chart gives the overall picture of vowel elision patterns, including labial prosodic features (see §3.2).

		V₂								
		i	ị	u	ụ		e	ẹ	o	ọ	a
	i	i	ị	u	ụ		e	ẹ	o	ọ	a
	ị	i	ị	u	ụ		e	ẹ	o	ọ	a
	u	u	u	u	u		ʷe	ʷẹ	ʷo	ʷọ	ʷa
	ụ	u	u	u	ụ		ʷe	ʷẹ	ʷo	ʷọ	ʷa
V₁	e	i	ị	u	ụ		e	ẹ	o	ọ	a
	ẹ	i	ị	u	ụ		e	ẹ	o	ọ	a
	o	i	ị	u	ụ		e	ẹ	o	ọ	a
	ọ	i	ị	u	ụ		e	ẹ	o	ọ	a
	a	i	ị	u	ụ		e	ẹ	o	ọ	a

Syntactic Junctures 55

From the above chart we observe that:
(a) in all combinations where both V_1 and V_2 are vowels of the close set *(i, i̱, u, u̱)*,
   (i) raised vowels *(i, u)* dominate nonraised vowels *(i̱, u̱)*;
   (ii) backness dominates frontness.

(b) In all combinations where V_1 and/or V_2 is a vowel of the nonclose set *(e, e̱, o, o̱, a)*, V_2 always dominates V_1

Harmony of the subject (preverb) pronoun

It will be observed from the examples in the preceding sections that in the grammatical structure PRONOUN + VERB + NOUN OBJECT, the pronoun vowel harmonizes with the vowel of the verb. Even when the vowel of the verb is lost by elision, the pronoun continues to harmonize with that underlying vowel, irrespective of the harmony set of the noun. In the normal running pronunciation, therefore, any harmonic similarity between the pronoun and the new combination of verb + noun object is accidental, the pronoun in some cases being in harmony, and in other cases out of harmony.

The phonological notation can be stated thus:

```
        Pr Vb                    N obj
H a/b    [(V CV)]      +   H a/b   [(VCV)]   =
H a/b    [(V)]         +   H a/b [(CVCV)]
```

3.2 Labial Syllable Prosody

A syllable prosody is a feature which characterizes a whole syllable, rather than one specific element of that syllable.

The syllables /tu/ and /du̱/, for example, are characterized by lip rounding for the consonants as much as for the vowels. Indeed, in the junction forms this prosody is maintained by the lip rounding for the consonant even when the vowel is elided. This applies to all -Cu and -Cu̱ examples, whatever the C, when followed by a nonclose vowel. Labial prosody is represented by *w* in the elision forms.

U as V_1 in VP + NP structures

tu + *e* > *twe*   *tú* + *ezí* > *twézí*
                            beat   children
                            ô twézí
                            'He beat the children.'

tu + ẹ > twẹ   tú + ẹvụ́ > twẹ́vụ́
beat goat
ô twẹ́bụ́
'He beat a goat.'

tu + o > two   tú + ozí > twózí
beat child
ô twózí
'He beat a child.'

tu + ọ > twọ   tú + ọ̀zà > twọ́zà
beat person
ô twọ́zà
'He beat a person.'

tu + a > twa   tú + àzà > twázà
beat people
ô twázà
'He beat people.'

dụ + e > dwe   dụ + ezì > dwezí
chase children
ộ dwezi
'He chased the children away.'

dụ + ẹ > dwẹ   dụ + ẹvú > dwẹvú
chase goat
ộ dwẹvụ́
'He chased a goat (away).'

dụ + o > dwo   dụ + ozí > dwozí
chase child
ộ dwozí
'He chased a child (away).'

dụ + ọ > dwọ   dụ + ọ̀zà > dwọ̀zà
chase person
ộ dwọ̀zà
'He chased a person (away).'

dụ + a > dwa   dụ + àzà > dwàzà
chase people
ộ dwàzà
'He chased people (away).'

Syntactic Junctures

We can represent these examples in the following phonological notation.

$^{w}(CV_1)$ + (V_2) > $^{w}(CV_2)$

U as V_1 in (N + N) NP structure

When /u/ and /ụ/ occur as V_1 in N + N COMPLEX NP structure they manifest exactly the same labial syllable prosody as in VP + NP listed above. (This confirms the regularity of labial syllable prosody resulting from /u/ and /ụ/ in the environment of nonclose vowels in the language.) Examples where /u/ and /ụ/ occur as V_1 are given in (N + N) NP structures and in a larger structure of NPs + VP + NPo.

```
ụ  +  ọ  >  wọ      evụ́ + ọ̀mụ̀yà   >   evwọ́mụ̀yà
                    goat + Omuya       goat (of) Omuya
                    [N   +   N]        'Omuya's goat'
                         NP
```

NP + VP structure:

```
evụ́ + ọ̀mụ̀yà  +  ọ̀ rí + enụ  +  ọ̀mụ́ha
[goat  Omuya]    it ate  [yam +  Omuha]
   NPs       +    VP   +     NPo
```

The sentence in the elided form would be:

evwọ́mụ̀yà   ọ̀ rénwọ́mụ́ha
goat (of) Omuya it ate yam (of) Omuha
'Omuya's goat ate Omuha's yam.'

The syllables in boldface represent the rounding juncture prosody of the (N + N) NP structure.

3.3 Palatal Syllable Prosody

Like the labial syllable prosody, palatal syllable prosody occurs at morpheme or word junctions. But unlike the labial prosody it is limited to syl-lables beginning with one of the consonants /h/, /s/, and /z/, and occurring before front close vowels /i/ and /ị/ when these segments occur in CV words and such words come into juxtaposition with other words having nonclose initial vowels. When a word, having a CV sequence where the C is /h/, /s/ or /z/ and the V is /i/ or /ị/, is followed by a nonclose initial vowel in the next word, palatal prosody always occurs at the junction. In the case of /h/ + /i/ or /ị/ the prosodic feature /y/ is written immediately following it /hy/. In the cases of /s/ and /z/ + /i/ or /ị/, the palatal exponent of /i/ or /ị/ would give rise to allophonic variation /ʃ/ and /ʒ/ respectively. These are exemplified below.

/hi̩/ or /hi̥/ + nonclose vowels *e, o, a*

The structure VP + NP of the imperative and the indicative moods, is used in the examples.

VP /hi̩/ 'to buy'
or /hi̥/ 'to call'

Semantic constraints limit the choice of VP to /hi̩/ 'to buy', or /hi̥/ 'to call'. There are other sequences, /hi̩/ 'to sweep' and /hi̥/ 'to weave', and /hi̩/ 'to string (beads)'. These can only precede particular kinds of nouns and such nouns do not have nonclose initial vowels. However, the principle of palatal prosody would apply in any environment of /hi̩/ or /hi̥/ plus a nominal with a nonclose initial vowel.

Selected noun phrases are used to follow the VP in the following examples:

hi̩ + e > hye   hi̩ + ècè > hyècè
                buy + wine
                ô hyècè
                'He bought some wine.'

hi̩ + e̩ > hye̩   hi̩ + e̩za > hye̩za
                buy + beans
                ô hye̩za
                'He bought some beans.'

hi̥ + o > hyo   hí + ozí > hyózí
                call + child
                ô hyózí
                'He called the child.'

hi̥ + o̩ > hyo̩   hí + o̩mùyà > hyó̩mùyà
                call + Omuya
                ô hyò̩mùyà
                'He called Omuya.'

hi̩ + a > hya   hi̩ + ano̩ > hyano̩
                buy + salt
                ô hyano̩
                'He bought some salt.'

/si/ or /si̩/ + nonclose vowels *e, o, a*

/si/ or /si̩/ followed by a nonclose initial vowel in the next word gives rise to the allophonic variant [ʃ]. The following examples are written phonemically except that the phonetic symbol [ʃ] is used to indicate the fused form.

Syntactic Junctures

si + e > [ʃe]   sì + ezí > [ʃezí]
               look for + children
               [ôʃezí]
               'He looked for the children.'

si + e > [ʃe]   sì + ęza > [ʃęza]
               look for + beans
               [ôʃęza]
               'He looked for some beans.'

si + o > [ʃo]   sì + ozí > [ʃozí]
               look for + child
               [ôʃozí]
               'He looked for the child.'

si + o > [ʃǫ]   sì + ǫmùyà > [ʃǫmùyà]
               look for + Omuya
               [ôʃǫmùyà]
               'He looked for Omuya.'

si + a > [ʃa]   sì + anǫ́ > [ʃánǫ́]
               look for + some salt
               [ôʃanǫ]
               'He looked for salt.'

/zi/ or /zi̧/ + nonclose vowels e, o, a

Similarly, /zi/ or /zi̧/ in the environment of nonclose vowels gives rise to the allophonic variant [ʒ] at word junctions.

zi̧ + e > [ʒe]   zi̧ + ezí > [ʒezí]
                hurt + children   'hurt the children'
                (iręsú)   ô   ʒezí
                (head)   it   hurt + children
                'The children had headaches.'

zi̧ + ę > [ʒę]   zi̧ + ęnębę́ní > [ʒęnębę́ní]
                hurt + elder brother
                (iręsú)   ô ʒęnębę́ní
                'The elder brother had a headache.'

zi̧ + o > [ʒo]   zi̧ + ozí > [ʒozí]
                hurt + child
                (iręsú)   ô ʒozí
                'The child had a headache.'

zi + o > [ʒo]   zi   + ǫ̀mùyà > [ʒǫ̀mùyà]
                hurt + Omuya
                (iresú)   ǫ̂ ʒǫ̀mùyà
                'Omuya had a headache.'

zi + a > [ʒa]   zi   + àdáava > [ʒàdáava]
                hurt + Adaava
                'Adaava had a headache.'

/hi/, /si/, and /zi/ in (N + N) NP structure

All the examples given for /hi/, /si/, and /zi/ above are in VP + NP structure. It is pertinent to point out the same palatal prosodic rule would apply in (N + N) NP structure. One example each in which /hi/, /si/, /zi/ sequences occur in (N + N) NP structures will suffice to confirm the validity of the rule.

ohi   + ozí   > ohyózí   (see §3.5)
broom + child   broom (of) child
                 'the child's broom'

òsì   + ẹnu   > [òʃẹ́nu]   (see §3.5)
poker + yam   poker (of) yam
                'a poker for picking hot yams from the pot'

ozí   + ǫ̀mùyà > [oʒǫ́mùyà]   (see §3.5)
child + Omuya   child (of) Omuya
                 'Omuya's child'

/hi/, /si/, or /zi/ + close vowels, *i* and *u*

/hi/, /si/, or /zi/ followed by a close initial vowel in the next word does not manifest palatal jucture syllable prosody. Examine these examples:

hì + i > hi   hì   + ízé > hízé
                buy + ize
                ǫ̂ hízé
                'He bought an ize (grass cutter).'

hì + u > hu   hì   + ùrá > hùrá
                buy + pig
                ǫ̂ hùrá
                'He bought a pig.'

Syntactic Junctures

sì + *i* > *si*   *sì*   + *ìzé* > *sìzé*
                      look + Ize
                      ô sìzé
                      'He looked for Ize.'

sì + *u* > *su*   *sì*   + *ùrú* > *sùrú*
                      look + Uru
                      ô sùrú
                      'He looked for Uru.'

zi̩ + *i* > *zi*   *zi̩* + *ìzé* > *zìzé*
                      hurt + Ize
                      ộ zìzé
                      'It hurt Ize.'

zi̩ + *u* > *zu*   *zi̩* + *ùrú* > *zùrú*
                      hurt + Uru
                      ộ zùrú
                      'It hurt Uru.'

It can be observed that it is the normal rule of vowel elision of close vowels that operates in the above examples (see §3.1).

3.4 Tone Changes

When two vowels of successive syllables come into juxtaposition one of the vowels is elided and the other one retained as described in §3.1. Every syllable has a tone largely carried by the vowel in Ebira, and morphotonemic changes that occur differ from the patterns of the vowels described. The three level tones of the language exhibit varying dominant characteristics at word junctions.

These are exemplified below, using the imperative mood of the verbal piece of VP + NP$_O$ structure. This structure also illustrates the contractions of three syllable tones to two tones. The labels T_1 and T_2 are used to illustrate the pattern of tone changes at junctions. T_1 is the tone on the final syllable of the verb. T_2 is the tone of the initial syllable of the noun object.

High tone /´/ as T_1

When high tone occurs as T_1, it will always dominate T_2, regardless of the tone of T_2.

T₁   T₂

H + H > H   yí   + ípe   > yípe
             steal   + flute   steal reed flute
             [―   ― ―]   > [― ―]
             H   + H M   > H M

H + M > H   rí   + uye   > rúye
             eat   + meat   'eat meat'
             [―   ― ―]   > [― ―]
             H   + M M   > H M

H + L > H   rí   + ùzì   > rúzì
             eat   + vegetable   'eat boiled vegetable'
             [―   ― ―]   > [― ―]
             H   + L L   > H L

Mid tone /-/ as T₁

When mid tone occurs as T₁ any tone that may occur as T₂ will always dominate T₁.

M + H > H   du   + íze   > dúze
             chase   + íze   'chase the grass cutter'
             [―   ― ―]   > [― ―]
             M   + H M   > H M

M + M > M   du   + uye   > duye
             chase   + animal   'chase the animal'
             [―   ― ―]   > [― ―]
             M   + M M   > M M

M + L > L   na   + òzè   > nòzè
             open   + door   'open the door'
             [―   ― ―]   > [― ―]
             M   + L L   > L L

Low tone /ˋ/ as T₁

Similarly, when low tone occurs as T₁, any tone that may occur as T₂ will dominate T₁.

L + H > H   hì   + ípe   > hípe
             buy   + flute   'buy a reed flute'
             [―   ― ―]   > [― ―]
             L   + H M   > H M

Syntactic Junctures

```
L  +  M  >  M      dà        +  eni          >  deni
                   fetch     +  water           'fetch water'
                   [—           — —]         >  [— —]
                   L         +  M M          >  M M

L  +  L  >  L      nè        +  ẹpẹ̀         >  nẹ̀pẹ̀
                   cook      +  soup           'cook the soup'
                   [—           — —  ]      >  [— —]
                   L         +  L L          >  L L
```

A summary chart of the three level tones at junctions

The chart in this section gives the overall summary of the shifting and dominance of the three level tones at word junctions.

		T_2		
		H	M	L
	H	H	H	H
T_1	M	H	M	L
	L	H	M	L

We can observe from the chart that:

(a) High tone, whether it occurs as T_1 or as T_2, dominates other tones.

(b) T_2 dominates T_1 in all other cases.

Automatic downstep

When high tone as T_1 is followed by low tone as T_2, the high tone dominates but automatic downstep occurs when the tone on the following syllable is high. For example:

```
VP  +  NP        rí        +  ùrá         >  rúrá[1]     'eat pig (pork)'
                 H         +  L H         >  H' H
                 eat       +  pig

(N + N) NP       ozí       +  ìzé         >  ozí'zé      'Ize's child'
                 M H       +  L H         >  M H' H
                 child     +  Ize
```

---

[1] ['] after high tone denotes downstep.

The tone environment, H + LH → H'H, seems to be the only environment found yet where automatic downstep occurs. H'H is the same phonetically as H M.

High-falling tone [ˆ] at junctions

High-falling tone does not occur word initially except on the verb prefix, /ô/ or /ộ/, where the syllable may sometimes stand as an independent morpheme. High-falling tone normally occurs word finally and it may come into juxtaposition with other tones. When it occurs at morpheme or word junctions its high tonetic exponent is dominant, and it would dominate other tones just like the level high tone — either in VP + NP or (N + N) NP structure as shown below. The high-falling tone functions at junctions in exactly the same way as high tone.

VP + NP	kụ́râ	+	oyí	>	kụ́róyí
	cry (at)	+	thief		'cry at a thief'
	H HF	+	M H	>	H H H
	ộ kụ́róyí				'He shouted and/or clapped his hands at a thief who is caught.'

(N + N) NP	ópô	+	àri	>	ópári
	long drum	+	Ari		'Ari's long drum'
	H HF	+	L M	>	H H M

ópári   ô   zózà
long drum (of) Ari   it-is good
'Ari's long drum is good.'

Low-rising tone [ˇ] at junctions

It was mentioned earlier that low-rising tone very rarely occurs and has a limited distribution in the language. It occurs only on the monosyllabic verbs listed in §2.6. For that reason, it occurs only in VP + NP structure and it can occur only as T_1 and never as T_2. This is the only situation in the language where V_1 and V_2 are juxtaposed that vowels retain their VOCALIC character. When low-rising tone occurs as T_1, its tonetic exponents of low and high spread over the two vowels that are juxtaposed. The low tone exponent occurs on V_1 while the high tone exponent dominates the inherent tone of V_2. The VP /hě/ 'to be in possession of something by finding it' juxtaposes with nominals having initial high, mid, and low tones.

Syntactic Junctures

hĕ	+	ípe	>	hèípe	'find and possess reed flute'
find	+	flute			
LR	+	H M	>	L HM	
				ô hèípe	'He is in possession of the reed flute he found.'

hĕ	+	ẹnụ	>	hèẹ́nụ	'find and possess a yam'
find	+	yam			
LR	+	M M	>	L H M	
				ô hèẹ́nụ	'He is in possession of a yam he found.'

hĕ	+	ùnọ	>	hèúnọ	'find and possess a cow'
find	+	cow			
LR	+	L M	>	L H M	
				ô hèúnọ	'He is in possession of a cow he found'.

3.5 High Tone as a Syntactic Juncture Feature

High tone is used to mark a genitive relationship and a locative relationship between two nominals. The genitive high tone can occur only in an NP + NP structure. The locative high tone can occur in an NP + NP structure as well as in VP + NP structure. These are described below giving some emphasis to syntactic demarcative features as well.

The genitive high tone

The genitive relationship between two nominals is marked by a high tone on the initial syllable of the second nominal. Thus irrespective of the inherent tones of V_1 and V_2, this genitive high tone dominates. Most nouns can occur in genitival relationship with other nouns.

NOUN₁		NOUN₂		GENITIVE NP	
ozí	+	ìzé		ozízé	
M H	+	L H		M H' H	
child	+	Ize		'Ize's child'	
ẹnụ	+	ozí		enʷózí	
M M	+	M H		M H H	
yam	+	ozí		'the child's yam'	
òsì	+	ẹnụ		òʃẹ́nụ	
L L	+	M M		L H M	
poker	+	yam		'the poker (of) for yam'	

ịpá	+	ècè	ịpécè
M H	+	L L	M H L
cup	+	wine	'the cup of wine'
ọhá	+	íze	ọhíze
M H	+	H H	M H M
spear	+	grasscutter	'spear of grasscutter, i.e., a spear for hunting grasscutter'
ípé	+	ozí	ípózí
H H	+	M H	H H H
flute	+	child	'the child's flute'
ẹnụ	+	ídá	ẹnúdá
M M	+	H H	M H H
yam	+	Ida	'Ida's yam'
ècè	+	ídá	ècídá
L L	+	H H	L H H
wine	+	Ida	'Ida's wine'
ìdù	+	òhí	ìdʷóhí
L L	+	L H	L H H
lion	+	chief	'the chief's lion'

Thus we can posit that in addition to the grammatical function, high tone is an important syntactic juncture feature. It always supersedes other tones at such word junctions.

The locative high tone

The locative relationship between two nominals in a transitive clause is marked by a high tone on the initial syllable of the second nominal. Similar to the genitive high tone, the locative tone can occur on NP + NP structure. The distinction between the genitive high tone and the locative high tone is syntactrically and semantically determined. One main distinction is that the second nominal phrase carrying initial high tone in locative phrases is always a name of a place or a particular location whereas the second nominal phrase of the genitive can be any noun.

Syntactic Junctures

```
VP        +   NP1    +   NP2
ộ hị̀    +   enụ    +   àgéva
HF L      +   M M    +   L H M
he buy    +   yam    +   Ageva
```

ộ   hyẹnụ ágéva
HF M M H H M
'He bought yam at Ageva.'

Note that the locative high tone replaces the low tone of initial syllable [à-] of àgéva in NP2, therefore giving rise to automatic downstep.

```
ộ       ná  +  íze    +   òhù
HF   +   H   +  H M    +   L L
he   +   sell+  grass- +   market
                cutter
```

ộ   níze óhù
HF H   M H L
'He sold a grass cutter in the market.'

The first noun is the direct object of the verb and the second noun is a locative and may be considered as a separate phrase.

There may be a natural pause between NP1 and NP2 in the above structures, and no vowel elision takes place between the two vowels that come into juxtaposition.

There is a class of verbs which takes a locative phrase directly without any other NP preceding the LP. These are verbs in which there is a relationship with a specific location implied. These include verbs like,

[rá]   'to live in or inhabit a place'
[z^{w}è] 'to run in a race at a place'
[gé]   'to meet at a place'

```
VP              NP₀ Loc

ộ  rá     + abá      ộ rábá
HF H      + M H      HF H H
he live   + Aba      'He lived in Aba.'

ộ  z$^w$è + èkó      ộ zwékó
HF L      + L H      HF H H
he run    + Eko      'He ran (a race) at Eko.'
```

ê gé   +   ègé   ê gégé
HF H   +   L H   HF H H
they meet +   Ege   'They met at Ege.'

Similar to the genitive tone, the locative high tone, in addition to its grammatical function, marks a syntactic junction. The junctions between *eṇu* and *àgéva; íze* and *òhù; rá* and *abá; zwè* and *èkó;* and *gé* and *ègé* in the above sentences are marked by high tone.

We can conclude therefore from these observations that high tone is a dominant tone, carrying heavy lexical, grammatical, and juncture functions in Ebira.

4 The Verbal Piece: Phrase Rank

4.1 The Verbal Piece

The term VERBAL PIECE is well known in linguistic studies, but is often used in slightly different ways. In this study VERBAL PIECE is used to cover any grammatical unit (at whatever rank) that has a verb as its nucleus. This use enables me to treat various categories of the verbal clause, the verbal phrase, the verbal group, and the verbal word. The description of the verbal piece in Ebira covers a very large part of the grammar of the language. It is the core of the grammar.

4.2 The Grammatical Hierarchy

For descriptive purposes, a grammatical hierarchy comprising various units is established. The units are sentence, clause, phrase, and word. Each unit is made up of units of the next lower rank. Thus a sentence unit consists of clauses, a clause unit consists of phrases, and a phrase unit consists of words.

Sentence rank

The structure of the sentence unit can be diagrammed as follows:

$$S \rightarrow \pm DepCl^3 + IndCl \pm Dep\ Cl^3$$

The sentence normally contains one obligatory independent clause, also called the main clause, one or more optional clauses before the independent clause, and one or more optional clause after the independent clause. Up to three dependent clauses may occur in sequence but usually not more than one occurs.

(a) // Ọmụ̀yà ọ̀ọ́   mẹ̀ ukọ́rọ   ẹ̀tẹ̀rẹ̀ /
    Omuya he-if do work   well/hard

   ộ vâ ɲí ẹ̀kẹ̀hị̀ //
   he will have money
   'If Omuya works hard, he will be rich.'

(b) // Ọmụ̀yà àà   me   ukọ́rọ ẹ̀tẹ̀rẹ̀ /
    Omuya he-is doing work well/hard

   ḿ   mè ré é //
   when I see him
   'Omuya was working hard when I saw him.'

Sentence (a) contains one dependent clause before the main clause whereas sentence (b) contains one dependent clause after the main clause. Conditional dependent clauses usually precede the main clause, but purpose and reason dependent clauses usually follow the main clause.

Clause rank (verbal clauses only)

The structure of the verbal clause consists of an obligatory verbal phrase, optional nominal subject and optional nominal object. It can be diagrammed as:

Verbal Clause → ± NP_S + VP ± NP_O

While NP_S is described here as optional, whether or not a given clause will include an NP_S, will depend on:

(1) the mood of the clause: imperative clauses never include an NP_S;

(2) the discourse structure: for example, where a sequence of clauses share the same NP_S, this will usually occur only in the first clause of the sequence.

Similarly, whether or not a given clause includes an NP_O is determined by two factors:

(1) the nature of the verb in the VP: for example, transitive verbs are usually followed by NP_O, intransitive verbs are never followed by NP_O (see further, §5.5);

(2) the discourse structure of the text: for example, in serial verb constructions, more than one verb may share the same NP_O, and this will occur only in the first clause of the series, although its presence is implied in subsequent clauses. (See chapter 6 for serial verb constructions.)

The Verbal Piece: Phrase Rank

Expansion of the clause consists of optional temporal phrase, or adverbial phrase, or locative phrase. (See further description in chapter 5.)

Phrase rank

There are several types of phrase units. These are:

Nominal phrase
Verbal phrase
Adverbial phrase
Temporal phrase
Locative phrase

The focus of this description is the verbal phrase. The structure of other types of phrases is described only to the extent that is necessary to explain the verbal piece.

4.3 The Verbal Phrase

The verbal phrase is the nucleus of the clause. The nucleus of the verbal phrase is the verb word, which is obligatory and constant in form. Every verbal phrase contains a verb word.

The structure of the verbal phrase

Grammatical changes such as difference of mood, tense, number, person, and polarity are signalled by the use of preverbal items, some of which are words; others are affixes. Preverbs also signal some dependent or independent relationships in the clause. These preverbs vary in tone and phonetic shape. In particular, their form is governed by the vowel harmony set of the verb which they qualify. Thus if the vowel of the verb word belongs to vowel harmony set A, the vowels of all its preverbs also belong to set A.

Up to three preverbs may occur in a verbal phrase, and preverbs are therefore grouped according to ORDERS, showing the order in which they will occur when they cooccur in the same VP. Order 1 preverbs occur first, followed by order 2 preverbs, followed by order 3 preverbs, followed by the verb. There are, however, a number of cooccurrence restrictions, which will be described below.

(a)   ó   yí̠   vâ   vé̠
Order 1   2   3   V
       3s   neg   fut   verb
       he   not   will   come
       'He will not come.'

(b)   ọ́   yị́   vâ   ná   á
Order 1   2   3   V   post v
         3s   neg   fut   verb   pron obj
         he   not   will   sell   it
'He will not sell it.'

Grammatical categories found in the verbal phrase in independent clauses are summarized on page 73. In brief, these are signalled by the different orders of preverbs as follows:

ORDER 1 SIGNALS	ORDER 2 SIGNALS	ORDER 3 SIGNALS
Tense: Past-simple, Progressive, Habitual Person: 1st, 2nd, 3rd Number: Singular and Plural	Polarity: Negative or Tense: Perfective	Tense: Future, Immediate or General

Thus person and number are signalled by preverbs of order 1, polarity by preverbs of order 2, while the differences of tense may be signalled by preverbs of any of the three orders in particular cases.

Order 1 preverbs are prefixes and are phonologically bound to the verb or to any preverb which they precede, although in the orthography they are written as separate words.

Another element of the VP is the pronoun object, a POSTVERB which is a suffix to the verb word. See example (b) above. The form of the pronoun object is also governed by the vowel harmony set of the verb.

Thus the structure of the verbal phrase may be diagrammed as follows:

VP → + PREVERB1 ± PREVERB2 ± PREVERB3 + V ± POSTVERB

All verbal phrases have an obligatory verb item, and (except for the imperative) an obligatory order 1 preverb. These structures account for all 1st, 2nd, and 3rd person singular and plural examples in the past-simple, progressive, and habitual positive tenses. Negative examples have the additional order 2 negative preverb. Perfective and future tense examples have the appropriate order 2 or order 3 preverbs.

The Verbal Piece: Phrase Rank

Summary of grammatical categories signalled in the verbal phrase in independent clauses

The following display summarizes the grammatical categories that are signalled in the verbal phrase:

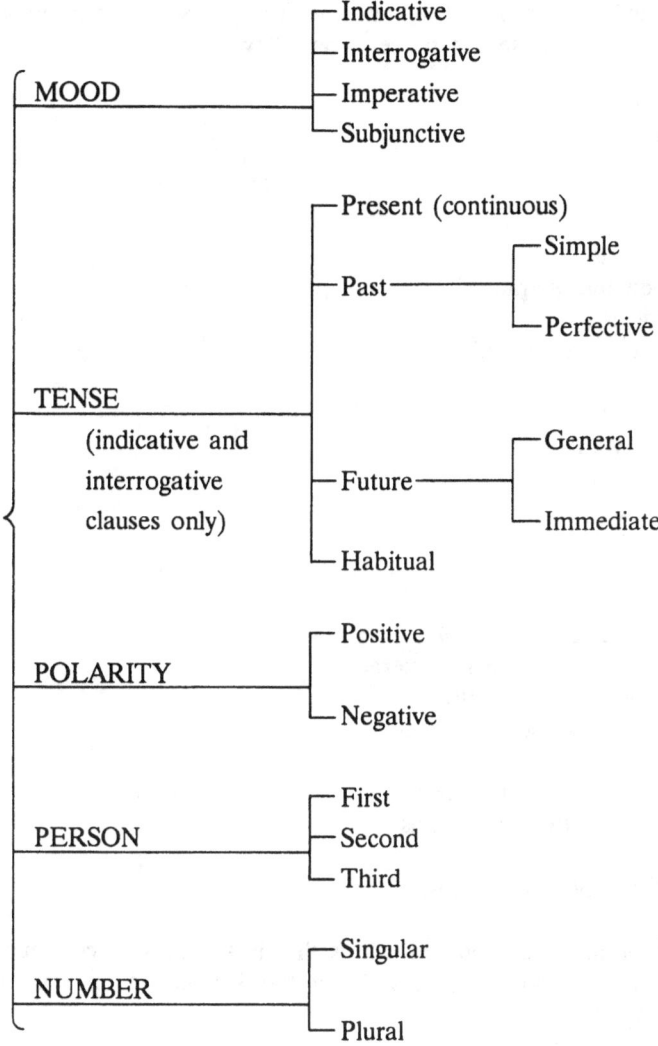

Note that there are no gender distinctions in the grammatical categories of the VP.

If one took full account of high register as a feature of interrogative pieces, it might be possible to consider mood as a category not of the verbal phrase but of the whole verbal clause. Here, however, mood is taken as a category of the verbal phrase since there are distinctive features for mood within the verbal phrase. (See §4.5 for the definition of high register.)

There is concord within the clause with respect to number and person between the noun phrase subject (NPs) and the verb phrase (VP) determined by the NPs and marked by sets of preverbs as follows:

Singular: *o, ọ,* and *a*
Plural: *e, ẹ,* and (*a*)

Singular:

    ocu ô ré ekú
    Ocu he see masquerade
    NP$_S$ + VP NP$_O$
    'Ocu saw the masquerade.'

    ocu ộ ná ẹnụ
    Ocu he sell yam
    NP$_S$ + VP NP$_O$
    'Ocu sold some yams.'

Plural:

    ocu onịrị oke ê ré ekú
    Ocu and Oke they see masquerade
    NP$_S$ + VP NP$_O$
    'Ocu and Oke saw the masquerade.'

    ocu onịrị oke ẹ́ ná ẹnụ
    Ocu and Oke they sell yams
    NP$_S$ + VP NP$_O$
    'Ocu and Oke sold some yams.'

The only exception to the concord rule is that in the present continuous tense of the indicative mood the preverb for the 3rd person singular and plural is the same, *àà*.

Singular:

> *ocu   àà   vẹ́*
> Ocu he-is coming
> NP_S   +   VP
> Ocu is coming.'

Plural:

> *ocu   oniṛi   oke   àà   vẹ́*
> Ocu and   Oke (he-is) coming
> NP_S   +   VP
> 'Ocu and Oke are coming.'

More examples of concord can be observed in chapter 5 where clause rank is discussed.

Any given verbal phrase exemplifies one option from each of the sets of options listed above. Thus a VP will be either indicative, interrogative, imperative, or subjunctive. A given indicative or interrogative VP will also be either present continuous, past, future, positive, or negative; also either first, second, or third person; and either singular or plural.

There are a number of cooccurrence restrictions in the selections of these options, and these will be described below.

Figures 1 to 4 below (§4.4) display the specific sets of preverbs which express each of these categories in the VP, and also (Figure 4) the preverbs which signal some dependent clause relationships.

Figure 1 displays the preverbs which signal tense options.
Figure 2 displays the preverbs which signal mood options.
Figure 3 displays the preverbs which signal negative polarity.
Figure 4 displays the preverbs which signal dependent clause relationships.

For each figure, there are two variant forms, vowel harmony set A and vowel harmony set B. As described earlier, it is the vowel harmony set of the verb that determines the harmony set of all the preverbs in any VP.

Person and number categories are displayed on the figures as they interplay with other categories. Sometimes preverbs signalling person and number fuse with other preverbs.

> *ḿ méé hú*
> PREV$_1$ + V
> am I + drink
> 'Am I drinking?'

In the preverb *ḿ méé* it is not possible to say which part is person, which part is number and which part is tense. There are more preverbs of this structure in the Figures.

Indicative mood, positive polarity and independent clause relationship are taken as the basic unmarked form of the VP.

4.4 Tense

Figure 1 shows how preverbs signal different options in indicative, positive verbal phrases. It is significant that the range of tense options which occur in interrogative verbal phrases and also in negative indicative verbal phrases is different from the tense options in indicative positive verbal phrases. These are displayed respectively in Figure 2 (for interrogative) and Figure 3 (for negative).

There are no contrastive tense options for either the imperative or subjunctive moods.

Points of interest

1. Note that the contrast between harmony set A preverbs and harmony set B preverbs in the Figures is not purely phonological. One might have expected that first person singular set B would be *mẹẹ;* however, instead the form which occurs is *maa*. Some forms, however, are purely phonologically conditioned. A study of all four Figures of the preverbs shows that the following rules apply:

    | *i / ị* | is always phonologically predictable, |
    | *u / ụ* | is always phonologically predictable, |
    | *o / ọ* | is always phonologically predictable, |
    | but *e* | may pair with *ẹ* (phonological) or with *a* (morphological) |

    Note that *a* never occurs in set A preverbs. In preverbs, *a* only occurs in the set B counterpart of preverbs which have the vowel *e* in set A. Thus in preverbs there are really only four vowel oppositions, as opposed to five oppositions in all other word classes and positions. See the comment in §2.3 on the ambivalence of *a*.

2. From the above it may be seen that the preverbs in Ebira are extremely complex. In this description I do not attempt to explain everything. A comparative study of related languages might give insight on the historical origin of the present forms, but such a study is outside the scope of this synchronic description.

3. Note that the preverb for the 2nd person is the same for singular and plural, *we/wa*. *nịnị* is a plural marker that is always added after the

verb when the 2nd person subject is plural to distinguish it from the 2nd person singular.

nịnị is not a part of any preverb, and it is independent of the intravowel harmony sequences of the VP. It always occurs after the VP and the object of the VP, hence the dots between the VP and *nịnị* in all the Figures. Pluralization will be described in full in §4.8.

4. As shown in Figure 1, there are tone classes of verbs, and tone has been discussed in detail in §2.6.

Present continuous tense

The order 1 preverb which signals the present continuous tense in the VP is *mèè* (1s) for harmony set A verbs, and *màà* (1s) for harmony set B verbs.

Set A
    mèè   *hú*
    I am drink
    I am drinking.

Set B
    màà *ná*
    I am sell
    I am selling.

A paradigm of the present continuous tense preverbs in the VP is given below:

Set A
mèè hú	'I am drinking'
wèè hú	'you (sg) are drinking'
èè hú	'he is drinking'
yèè hù	'we are drinking'
wèè hú nịnị	'you (pl) are drinking'
éyée hú	'they are drinking'

Set B
màà ná	'I am selling'
wàà ná	'you (sg) are selling'
àà ná	'he is selling'
yàà ná	'we are selling'
wàà ná nịnị	'you (pl) are selling'
eyàà ná	'they are selling'

Figure 1. Tense (Indicative Mood)—Harmony Set A

	1st Person Singular	2nd Person Singular	3rd Person Singular	1st Person Plural	2nd Person Plural	3rd Person Plural	Tone
Present Continuous	mèè	wèè	èè	yèè	wèè . . . nịnị	é yée	L L (H M H)
Past Simple	mê	wê	ô	yê	wê . . . nịnị	ê	HF
Past Perfective	mé sí	wé sí	ó sí	yé sí	wé sí . . . nịnị	é sí	H H
Past Perfective	mé rée	wé rée	ó rée	yé rée	wé rée . . . nịnị	é rée	H M H
Future General	mi vê	u vê	o vê	i vê	u vê . . . nịnị	e vê	M HF
Future Immediate	mèè vê	wèè vê	èè vê	yèè vê	wèè vê . . . nịnị	é yée vê	L L HF / H M HF
Habitual	mịị	uụ	oọ	ịị	uụ . . . nịnị	eẹ	M M

Figure 1. Tense (Indicative Mood)—Harmony Set B

	1st Person Singular	2nd Person Singular	3rd Person Singular	1st Person Plural	2nd Person Plural	3rd Person Plural	Tone
Present Continuous	màà	wàà	àà	yàà	wàà . . . nìnì	ę́yáa	L L (H H' H)
Past Simple	mâ	wâ	ô	yâ	wâ . . . nìnì	ê	HF
Past Perfective	má sí	wá sí	ǫ́ sí	yá sí	wá sí . . . nìnì	ę́ sí	H H
Past Perfective	má ráa	wá ráa	ǫ́ ráa	yá ráa	wá ráa . . . nìnì	ę́ráa	H M H
Future General	mị̀ vá	ụ̀ vá	ǫ̀ vá	ị̀ vá	ụ̀ vá . . . nìnì	ẹ̀ vá	M HF
Future Immediate	màà vá	wàà vá	àà vá	yàà vá wàà vá . . . nìnì ę́ yáa vá			L L HF (H M H)
Habitual	mị̀ị̀	ụ̀ụ̀	ǫ̀ǫ̀	ị̀ị̀	ụ̀ụ̀ . . . nìnì	ẹ̀ẹ̀	M M

The past perfective preverb has two forms, the particles *rée* or *ráa* and *sí* or *sị́*. Both forms denote perfective and both are in current use. They can be used interchangeably in most contexts by the same speaker. The only distinction which occurs in their use is described in §4.4.

Simple past tense

Although this tense has usually been named simple past because it most frequently has past meaning, in fact, it can also have present meaning in some contexts. There is no contrast between past and present in Ebira in the simple form of the VP. Distinctions of time are indicated by other expressions, such as temporals. *mê hú* 'I drink' could mean *mê 'hú (eyíneyíni)* 'I drink (every day)' or *mê hú (èèrí)* 'I drank (yesterday).' The order 1 preverb which signals this tense in the VP is *mê* for '1st person singular' for set A and *mâ* for '1st person singular' for set B.

Set A

mê	hú		'I drank'
wê	hú		'you (sg) drank'
ô	hú		'he drank'
yê	hú		'we drank'
wê	hú	nịnị	'you (pl) drank'
ê	hú		'they drank'

Set B

mâ	nà		'I tore'
wâ	nà		'you (sg) tore'
ộ	nà		'he tore'
yâ	nà		'we tore'
wâ	nà	nịnị	'you (pl) tore'
ê	nà		'they tore'

Past perfective tense

The past perfective tense is signalled by two preverbs. These are preverbs of orders 1 and 2.

Preverb order 1 is *mé* and order 2 is *sí* or *rée* for set A.
Preverb order 1 is *má* and order 2 is *sị* or *ráa* for set B.

There are two forms of the preverb particle denoting perfective both in sets A and B. There does not seem to be any distinction in meaning between either of these order 2 particles. The same speaker may use them interchangeably.

There is, however, a difference of form in the way that the two particles are used in the past perfective tense. *mé sí hú* or *mé rée hú* both mean 'I have drunk.'

In a VP where there is a pronominal object or a nominal object, the object normally follows the verb. However, when the perfective particle *sí/sị* is used the object may precede the verb as in the following examples:

The Verbal Piece: Phrase Rank

mé	sí	ècè	hú	and	mé sí	ó	hú
I	have	wine	drunk		I have	it	drunk

'I have drunk wine.' 'I have drunk it.'

Note that the form of the preverb *sí* is still governed by the vowel harmony set of the verb, even though it is separated from it by the pronominal object of NP$_O$.

When perfective particle *rée/ráa* is used, the object never precedes the verb.

me rée hú ǫ́   ma ráa rí́ ǫ́
I have drunk it   I have eat it
'I have drunk it.' 'I have eaten it.'

The paradigm for the past perfective tense follows:

Set A

mé	sí	hú		'I have drunk'
wé	sí	hú		'you (sg) have drunk'
ó	sí	hú		'he has drunk'
yé	sí	hú		'we have drunk'
wé	sí	hú	nịnị	'you (pl) have drunk'
é	sí	hú		'they have drunk'

mé	rée	hú		'I have drunk'
wé	rée	hú		'you (sg) have drunk'
ó	rée	hú		'he has drunk'
yé	rée	hú		'we have drunk'
wé	rée	hú	nịnị	'you (pl) have drunk'
é	rée	hú		'they have drunk'

Set B

má	sị́	nà		'I have torn'
wá	sị́	nà		'you (sg) have torn'
ọ́	sị́	nà		'he has torn'
yá	sị́	nà		'we have torn'
wá	sị́	nà	nịnị	'you (pl) have torn'
ẹ́	sị́	nà		'they have torn'

má	ráa	ná	'I have sold'
wá	ráa	ná	'you (sg) have sold'
ọ́	ráa	ná	'he has sold'
yá	ráa	ná	'we have sold'

wá	ráa	ná	nịnị	'you (pl) have sold'
ẹ́	ráa	ná		'they have sold'

Future tense

Ebira distinguishes between two forms of the future: general future and immediate future. The general future refers to any time from the moment of speaking until indefinite time in the future. It could be the next hour, the next day, the next month or many years to come. Events or things referred to in the general future may or may not happen.

On the other hand, the immediate future refers to time that is definite and not too far away. Events referred to in the immediate future tense are most likely to happen within a foreseeable definite time. Usually there are signs or some evidence which suggest some degree of certainty.

Both general future and immediate future are signalled by two preverbs. They differ in order 1 preverb but the order 3 preverb is the same for both.

General future. General future is signalled by the preverbs: order 1 *mí* (1s) and order 3 *vê* for set A harmony words; order 1 *mị́* (1s) and order 3 *vâ* for set B harmony words.

Set A

mí	vê	hú		'I will drink'
ú	vê	hú		'you (sg) will drink'
ó	vê	hú		'he will drink'
í	vê	hú		'we will drink'
ú	vê	hú	nịnị	'you (pl) will drink'
é	vê	hú		'they will drink'

Set B

mị́	vâ	ná		'I will sell'
ụ́	vâ	ná		'you (sg) will sell'
ọ́	vâ	ná		'he will sell'
ị́	vâ	ná		'we will sell'
ụ́	vâ	ná	nịnị	'you (pl) will sell'
ẹ́	vâ	ná		'they will sell'

Immediate future. The immediate future is signalled in the VP by the preverbs: order 1 *mèè* (1s) and order 3 *vê* for set A harmony verbs; and order 1 *màà* (1s) and order 3 *vâ* for set B harmony verbs.

Set A

mèè	vê	hú	'I am about to drink'
wèè	vê	hú	'you (sg) are about to drink'

èè	vê	hú		'he is about to drink'
yèè	vê	hú		'we are about to drink'
wèè	vê	hú	nini	'you (pl) are about to drink'
e yéé	vê	hú		'they are about to drink'

Set B

màà	vâ	ná		'I am about to sell'
wàà	vâ	ná		'you (sg) are about to sell'
àà	vâ	ná		'he is about to sell'
yàà	vâ	ná		'we are about to sell'
wàà	vâ	ná	nini	'you (pl) are about to sell'
e yáá	vâ	ná		'they are about to sell'

Habitual tense

The habitual tense in Ebira denotes actions which are performed regularly and have become the habit of the individuals concerned. This tense represents what may be translated in English as, 'usually', 'normally', or 'habitually'. The tense is signalled in the VP by preverb order 1 only, which is *mii* (1s) for harmony set A verbs and *mii* (1s) for harmony set B verbs.

This is the only tense that carries mid tone and mid tone only in the preverbs in all its forms.

Set A

mii	hú		'I habitually drink'
uu	hú		'you (sg) habitually drink'
oo	hú		'he habitually drinks'
ii	hú		'we habitually drink'
uu	hú	nini	'you (pl) habitually drink'
ee	hú		'they habitually drink'

Set B

mii	ná		'I habitually sell'
uu	ná		'you (sg) habitually sell'
oo	ná		'he habitually sells'
ii	ná		'we habitually sell'
uu	ná	nini	'you (pl) habitually sell'
ee	ná		'they habitually sell'

4.5 Mood

The indicative mood has already been illustrated in Figure 1, where all the examples are indicative. Figure 2 shows how preverbs signal different options in the verbal phrase for the other moods.

Figure 2. Mood—Harmony Set A

	1st Person Singular	2nd Person Singular	3rd Person Singular	1st Person Plural	2nd Person Plural	3rd Person Plural	Tone
Present Continuous	ḿ méé	ú w é	é éé	í yéé	ú wéé . . . nịnị	é yéé	H H'H
Simple Past	méé	wéé	óó	yéé	wéé . . . nịnị	éé	H H
Past Perfective	méé sí	wéé sí	óó sí	yéé sí	wéé sí . . . nịnị	éé sí	H H H
Future	méé vê	wéé vê	óó vê	yéé vê	wéé vê . . . nịnị	éé vê	H H HF
Habitual	m mée	u wée	o óo	i yée	u wée . . . nịnị	e ée	M H M
Imperative	#	#	#	#	#	#	#
Subjunctive	me	we	ò	ye	we . . . nịnị	è	M (L)

The Verbal Piece: Phrase Rank

Figure 2. Mood—Harmony Set B

	1st Person Singular	2nd Person Singular	3rd Person Singular	1st Person Plural	2nd Person Plural	3rd Person Plural	Tone
INTER Present Continuous	ḿ máá	ú̱ wáá	á áá	í̱ yáá	ú̱ wáá . . . ni̱ni̱	é yáá	H H'H H H'H
Simple Past	máá	wáá	ọ́ọ́	yáá	wáá . . . ni̱ni̱	ẹ́ẹ́	H H
Past Perfective	máá sí	wáá sí	ọ́ọ́ sí	yáá sí	wáá sí . . . ni̱ni̱	ẹ́ẹ́ sí	H H H
Future	máá vâ	wáá vâ	ọ́ọ́ vâ	yáá vâ	wáá vâ . . . ni̱ni̱	ẹ́ẹ́ vâ	H H HF
Habitual	m máa	ụ wáa	ọ ọ̀o	ị yáa	ụ wáa . . . ni̱ni̱	e ẹ̀e	M H M
Imperative	#	#	#	#	#	#	#
Subjunctive	ma	wa	ò	ya	wa . . ni̱ni̱	è	M (L)

As in the indicative mood, rée/ráa may occur as alternative to sí/sị́ in the past perfective tense.

The interrogative mood

The interrogative mood is also signalled by preverbs in the verbal phrase. All the tenses listed in Figure 1 may be used in the interrogative mood, except that there is only one form of the future, general future, with no contrast between general future and immediate future. This reflects the fact that immediate future always implies some degree of definiteness, a definite expectation that the action or event will happen, and this is semantically incompatible with the interrogative mood.

In addition to specific preverbs with high tone shown in Figure 2, high register is a feature of the interrogative mood. High register is defined as raising of the voice pitch above the normal pitch level when uttering a phrase or a sentence. The high pitch spreads over the entire phrase or utterance delimited by pauses.

The interrogative present continous tense. The interrogative mood in the present continuous tense is marked by a DOUBLE ORDER 1 preverb which is *ḿ méé* (1s) for harmony set A verbs and *ḿ máá* (1s) for harmony set B verbs.

A study of column one of Figure 2 and comparison with Figure 1 will show why the term DOUBLE ORDER 1 preverb is used here. When the order 1 preverb has a simple vowel in the indicative form, the interrogative is signalled (partially) by doubling that vowel.

	INDICATIVE ORDER 1 PREVERB (1s)	INTERROGATIVE ORDER 1 PREVERB (1s)
Simple Past:	*mê/mâ*	*méé/máá*
Past Perfective:	*mé/má*	*méé/máá*
General Future :	*mi/mi*	*méé/máá*

But when the preverb already has a double vowel in the indicative form:

Present Continuous:	*mèè/màà*	*ḿ méé/ḿ máá*
Habitual:	*mii/mii*	*ḿ mée/ḿ máa*

The interrogative is signalled (partially) by a syllabic prefix to the preverb, whose form is largely phonologically conditioned by the following sounds:

m-	before *m*		1s pres cont tense
u-/ụ-	before *w*		2s/2pl pres cont tense
e-/ẹ-	before *e/ẹ*		3p habitual tense
o-/ọ-	before *o/ọ*		3s habitual tense
e-	before *e*	(Ha)	3s pres cont tense
a-	before *a*	(Hb)	3s pres cont tense

i-/i̩	before y		1p pres cont tense
e-/e̩-	before y		3p pres cont tense

(Ha), (Hb) = harmony set A and harmony set B.

The paradigm examples for the interrogative present continuous tense follow. Since these forms are exclusively interrogative, there is no need to use a question mark in Ebira.

Set A

ḿ méé	hú		'am I drinking?'
ú wéé	hú		'are you (sg) drinking?'
é éé	hú		'is he drinking?'
í yéé	hú		'are we drinking?'
ú wéé	hú	ni̩ni̩	'are you (pl) drinking?'
é yéé	hú		'are they drinking?'

Set B

ḿ máá	ná		'am I selling?'
ú̩ wáá	ná		'are you (sg) selling?'
á áá	ná		'is he selling?'
í̩ yáá	ná		'are we selling?'
ú̩ wáá	ná	ni̩ni̩	'are you (pl) selling?'
é̩ yáá	ná		'are they selling?'

The interrogative simple past. The interrogative mood in the simple past tense is marked by order 1 preverb: *méé* (1s) for harmony set A verbs and *máá* (1s) for harmony set B verbs.

Set A

méé	hú		'did I drink?'
wéé	hú		'did you (sg) drink?'
óó	hú		'did he drink?'
yéé	hú		'did we drink?'
wéé	hú	ni̩ni̩	'did you (pl) drink?'
éé	hú		'did they drink?'

Set B

máá	ná		'did I sell?'
wáá	ná		'did you (sg) sell?'
ó̩ó̩	ná		'did he sell?'
yáá	ná		'did we sell?'
wáá	ná	ni̩ni̩	'did you (pl) sell?'
é̩é̩	ná		'did they sell?'

The interrogative past perfective. The interrogative mood in the past perfective is marked by order 1 and order 2 preverbs: *méé sí* (1s) for set A harmony verbs and *máá sị́* (1s) for set B harmony verbs.

Set A

méé sí	*hú*		'have I drunk?'
wéé sí	*hú*		'have you (sg) drunk?'
óó sí	*hú*		'has he drunk?'
yéé sí	*hú*		'have we drunk?'
wéé sí	*hú*	*ṇiṇi*	'have you (pl) drunk?'
éé sí	*hú*		'have they drunk?'

Set B

máá sị́	*ná*		'have I sold?'
wáá sị́	*ná*		'have you (sg) sold?'
ọ́ọ́ sị́	*ná*		'has he sold?'
yáá sị́	*ná*		'have we sold?'
wáá sị́	*ná*	*ṇiṇi*	'have you (pl) sold?'
ẹ́ẹ́ sị́	*ná*		'have they sold?'

The interrogative future. The interrogative mood in the future tense in the VP is just one form, the general future. It is signalled by order 1 and order 3 preverbs: *méé vê* (1s) for harmony set A verbs and *máá vâ* (1s) for harmony set B verbs.

Set A

méé vê	*hú*		'shall I drink?'
wéé vê	*hú*		'will you (sg) drink?'
óó vê	*hú*		'will he drink?'
yéé vê	*hú*		'shall we drink?'
wéé vê	*hú*	*ṇiṇi*	'will you (pl) drink?'
éé vê	*hú*		'will they drink?'

Set B

máá vâ	*ná*		'shall I sell?'
wáá vâ	*ná*		'will you (sg) sell?'
ọ́ọ́ vâ	*ná*		'will he sell?'
yáá vâ	*ná*		'shall we sell?'
wáá vâ	*ná*	*ṇiṇi*	'will you (pl) sell?'
ẹ́ẹ́ vâ	*ná*		'will they sell?'

The interrogative habitual. The interrogative mood in the habitual tense is marked in the VP by double order 1 preverb: *ḿ mée* (1s) for set A verbs and *ḿ máa* (1s) for set B verbs.

The Verbal Piece: Phrase Rank

Set A

m	mée	hú	'do I habitually drink?'
u	wée	hú	'do you (sg) habitually drink?'
o	óo	hú	'does he habitually drink?'
i	yée	hú	'do we habitually drink?'
u	wée	hú nini	'do you (pl) habitually drink?'
e	ée	hú	'do they habitually drink?'

Set B

m	máa ná		'do I habitually sell?'
u̱	wáa ná		'do you (sg) habitually sell?'
o̱	óo ná		'does he habitually sell?'
i̱	yáa ná		'do we habitually sell?'
u̱	wáa ná nini		'do you (pl) habitually sell?'
e̱	ée ná		'do they habitually sell?'

The imperative mood

The imperative mood in the VP has zero preverb and is tenseless. By its structure and semantics, it can occur with second person singular and plural only. It consists only of a verb in the VP, optionally followed by a pronoun object postverb.

SINGULAR	hú		'drink'
	hú o		'drink it'
PLURAL	hú	nini	'you (pl) drink'
	hú o	nini	'you (pl) drink it'

The imperative mood is a command addressed to a second person. Therefore any action verb can occur in the imperative mood. Stative verbs do not occur in the imperative mood.

The subjunctive mood

The subjunctive mood in the VP is similar to the imperative mood in that it is a mild command or a wish. It expresses meaning similar to the words 'should', 'ought to', or 'let' in English.

The mood is signalled by order 1 preverb: *me* (1s) for harmony set A verbs and *ma* (1s) for harmony set B verbs.

Set A

me	hú		'I should drink'
we	hú		'you (sg) should drink'
ò	hú		'he should drink'
ye	hú		'we should drink'
we	hú	nini	'you (pl) should drink'
è	hú		'they should drink'

Set B

ma	ná		'I should sell'
wa	ná		'you (sg) should sell'
ọ̀	ná		'he should sell'
ya	ná		'we should sell'
wa	ná	nịnị	'you (pl) should sell'
ẹ̀	ná		'they should sell'

Note that 3rd person singular and plural preverbs have low tone, while the others have mid tone.

4.6 Negative Polarity

Figure 3 shows how preverbs signal negative polarity in the verbal phrase in the indicative.

Negative indicative tenses

There are fewer tense options in negative indicative verbal phrases than in positive indicative verbal phrases. The tenses signalled by preverbs in the negative VP include only the simple past, the past perfective, general future, and habitual tenses.

I have given ample paradigms for Figures 1 and 2; therefore I will just give a harmony pair paradigm for each of the tenses in Figure 3.

The negative indicative: simple past. The negative indicative in the simple past tense is signalled by preverbs *mé yí* (1s) for harmony set A verbs and *mẹ́ yị́* (1s) for harmony set B verbs.

Set A

mé yí	hú		'did not drink'
wé yi	hú		'you (sg) did not drink'
ó yí	hú		'he did not drink'
yé yí	hú		'we did not drink'
wé yi	hú nini		'you (pl) did not drink'
é yi	hú		'they did not drink'

Set B

mẹ́	yí	ná	'I did not sell'
wẹ́	yí	ná	'you (sg) did not sell'
ọ	yí	ná	'he did not sell'
yẹ́	yí	ná	'we did not sell'
wẹ́	yí	ná	'you (pl) did not sell'
ẹ́	yí	ná	'they did not sell'

The negative indicative: past perfective. The negative indicative in past perfective tense is signalled by preverbs *méè yí* (1s) for harmony set A verbs and *mẹ́ẹ̀ yí* (1s) for harmony set B verbs.

Set A

méè yí	ré			'I have not seen'
wéè yí	ré			'you (sg) have not seen'
óò yí	ré			'he has not seen'
yéè yí	ré			'we have not seen'
wéè yí	ré	nịnị		'you (pl) have not seen'
éè yí	ré			'they have not seen'

Set B

mẹ́ẹ̀ yí	rị́			'I have not eaten'
wẹ́ẹ̀ yí	rị́			'you (sg) have not eaten'
ọ́ọ̀ yí	rị́			'he has not eaten'
yẹ́ẹ̀ yí	rị́			'we have not eaten'
wẹ́ẹ̀ yí	rị́	nịnị		'you (pl) have not eaten'
ẹ́ẹ̀ yí	rị́			'they have not eaten'

The negative indicative future. The negative indicative in future tense is signalled by preverbs *mé yí vê* (1s) for harmony set A verbs and *mẹ́ yí vâ* (1s) for harmony set B verbs.

Set A

mé yí vê	hú			'I will not drink'
wé yí vê	hú			'you (sg) will not drink'
ó yí vê	hú			'he will not drink'
yé yí vê	hú			'we will not drink'
wé yí vê	hú	nịnị		'you (pl) will not drink'
é yí vê	hú			'they will not drink'

Figure 3. Negative Polarity—Harmony Set A

	1st Person Singular	2nd Person Singular	3rd Person Singular	1st Person Plural	2nd Person Plural	3rd Person Plural	Tone
Simple Past	mé yí	wé yí	ó yí	yé yí	wé yí . . . nini	é yí	H H
Past Perfective	méè yí	wéè yí	òò yí	yéè yí	éè yì . . . nini	éè yí	H L H
Future	mé yí vê	wé yí vê	ó yí vê	yè yí vê	wé yí vê . . . nini	é yí vê	H H HF
Habitual	mé me	wé me	ó me	yé me	wé me . . . nini	é me	H M

Figure 3. Negative Polarity—Harmony Set B

	1st Person Singular	2nd Person Singular	3rd Person Singular	1st Person Plural	2nd Person Plural	3rd Person Plural	Tone
Simple Past	mẹ́ yị́	wẹ́ yị́	ọ́ yị́	yẹ́ yị́	wẹ́ yị́ . . . nịnị	ẹ́ yị́	H H
Past Perfective	mẹ́ẹ̀ yị́	wẹ́ẹ̀ yị́	ọ́ọ̀ yị́	yẹ́ẹ̀ yị́	wẹ́ẹ̀ yị́ . . . nịnị	ẹ́ẹ̀ yị́	HL H
Future	mẹ́ yị́ vâ	wẹ́ yị́ vâ	ọ́ yị́ vâ	yẹ́ yị́ vâ	wẹ́ yị́ vâ . . . nịnị	ẹ́ yị́ vâ	H H HF
Habitual	má ma	wá ma	ọ́ ma	yá ma	wá ma . . . nịnị	ẹ́ ma	H M

Negative is signalled basically by *yí-/yị́-*.

Comparison with Figure 1 shows the following points of interest:

(a) In the past perfective, the preverb *rée-/ráa-* is not used but there is apparent compensatory lengthening of the first preverb.
(b) In the habitual tense, a completely different form, *me/ma*, is used to signal negative.

Set B

mẹ́	yí	vâ	ná		'I will not sell'
wẹ́	yí	vâ	ná		'you (sg) will not sell'
ọ̀	yí	vâ	ná		'he will not sell'
yẹ́	yí	vâ	ná		'we will not sell'
wẹ́	yí	vâ	ná	nịnị	'you (pl) will not sell'
ẹ́	yí	vâ	ná		'they will not sell'

The negative indicative habitual. The negative indicative in the habitual tense is signalled by preverbs: *mé me* (1s) for harmony set A verbs and *má ma* (1s) for harmony set B verbs.

Set A

mé	me	hú	ịbíya		'I do not habitually drink beer'
wé	me	hú	ịbíya		'you (sg) do not habitually drink beer'
ó	me	hú	ịbíya		'he does not habitually drink beer'
yé	me	hú	ịbíya		'we do not habitually drink beer'
wé	me	hú	ịbíya	nịnị	'you (pl) do not habitually drink beer'
é	me	hú	ịbíya		'they do not habitually drink beer'

Set B

má	ma	rị́	ụ̀rá		'I do not habitually eat pork'
wá	ma	rị́	ụ̀rá		'you (sg) do not habitually eat pork'
ó	ma	rị́	ụ̀rá		'he does not habitually eat pork'
yá	ma	rị́	ụ̀rá		'we do not habitually eat pork'
wá	ma	rị́	ụ̀rá	nịnị	'you (pl) do not habitually eat pork'
ẹ́	ma	rị́	ụ̀rá		'they do not habitually eat pork'

Note that the negative order 2 preverbs for the habitual tense are *me/ma* whereas the preverbs *yí/yí* 'are used in other tenses.

The language employs the preverbs *me/ma* in the negative habitual to maintain the mid tone which is characteristic of the habitual tense since *yí/yí* negative preverbs always carry high tone.

Negative tenses in the interrogative mood

The negative tense in the interrogative mood is not signalled by preverbs in the VP but by another element of the VP which may be labelled a prosodic suffix of the VP. This prosodic suffix is lengthening of the final vowel of the VP which will carry a mid tone and is a syllable on its own. Generally any indicative VP can be made interrogative in Ebira by lengthening the final vowel, and the lengthened vowel will always carry mid tone. All the tenses which occur in the negative indicative VP could also occur in the negative interrogative VP. High register as a feature of the interrogative has already

The Verbal Piece: Phrase Rank 95

been mentioned (page 86). Just a few sets of examples are given below. (See §5.10 for further discussion.)

Simple Past:

Set A

mé yí	hú u		'did I not drink?'
wé yí	hú u		'did you (sg) not drink?'
ó yí	hú u		'did he not drink?'
yé yí	hú u		'did we not drink?'
wé yí	hú u	nịnị	'did you (pl) not drink?'
é yí	hú u		'did they not drink?'

Set B

mẹ yí	ná a		'did I not sell?'
wẹ yí	ná a		'did you (sg) not sell?'
ọ yí	ná a		'did he not sell?'
yẹ yí	ná a		'did we not sell?'
wẹ yí	ná a	nịnị	'did you (pl) not sell?'
ẹ yi	ná a		'did they not sell?'

Other tenses of the negative interrogative have paradigm examples similar to the above. The important point is that the final lengthened vowel always carries mid tone and constitutes an additional syllable.

Negative imperative mood

The negative imperative is formed by an initial *àsụ́* plus the verb. This *àsụ́* does not harmonize with any other forms; it remains invariable. It is difficult to classify it as a preverb, as it does not have the usual characteristics of preverbs. It cannot occur alone, and it occurs only as a way of making the negative imperative.

(2s) àsụ́   nâ   (2p) àsụ́   nâ   nịnị
     don't go   don't go   (pl)
     'don't go'   'you (pl) don't go'

Negative subjunctive mood

As in the negative imperative, negation is not signalled in the VP by a preverb. The negative subjunctive has a negative phrase similar to the negative imperative but longer in structure. This is followed by an order 1 preverb identical to those occurring in the positive subjunctive. See Figure 2. The negative phrase for the subjunctive is *àsụ́ zệ ka* 'don't let, or should not'.

Set A

àsú zẹ̀ ka	me hú			'don't let me drink'
àsú zẹ̀ ka	we hú			'don't [let you (sg)] drink'
àsú zẹ̀ ka	ò hú			'don't let him drink'
àsú zẹ̀ ka	ye hú			'don't let us drink'
àsú zẹ̀ ka	we hú	nịnị		'don't [let you (pl)] drink'
àsú zẹ̀ ka	è hú			'don't let them drink'

Set B

àsú zẹ̀ ka	ma ná			'don't let me sell'
àsú zẹ̀ ka	wa ná			'don't [let you (sg)] sell'
àsú zẹ̀ ka	ọ̀ ná			'don't let him sell'
àsú zẹ̀ ka	ya ná			'don't let us sell'
àsú zẹ̀ ka	wa ná	nịnị		'don't [let you (pl)] sell'
àsú zẹ̀ ka	ẹ̀ ná			'don't let them sell'

The negative phrases for the imperative and the subjunctive are not part of NP or part of VP. They are some of the neutral elements in the language which have syntactic functions but are not conveniently assigned to a particular unit.

4.7 Dependent Clauses

There are two dependent clause relationships which in Ebira are signalled by preverbs, unlike their English translations. These are IF and WHEN dependent clauses. Figure 4 displays these dependent clause preverbs.

Two dependent clause relationships are signalled by preverbs in the verbal phrase, IF dependent clause relationship and WHEN dependent clause relationships. Four tenses are signalled by preverbs in IF clause relationships. These are present continuous, simple past, past perfective, and general future. Two tenses are signalled in WHEN clause relationships which are present continuous and simple past tenses. Examples of dependent clauses are better presented in relationships with independent clauses. A set of examples in simple past tense are given for IF dependent clauses and another set of examples in simple past tense also is presented for WHEN dependent clauses.

Dependent clause IF

The preverb for IF dependent clause in the simple past tense in the VP is *mèé* (1s) for harmony set A verbs and *màá* (1s) for harmony set B verbs.

The Verbal Piece: Phrase Rank

Set A

(a) mèé húsè, mị̀ vâ dọ́
    I-if ask I will get
    'if I ask, I will get'

(b) wèé húsè, ụ vâ dọ́
    you (sg)–if ask you (sg) will get
    'if you (sg) ask, you (sg) will get'

(c) òó húsè, ọ vâ dọ́
    he-if ask he will get
    'if he asks, he will get'

(d) yèé húsè, ị vâ dọ́
    we-if ask we will get
    'if we ask, we will get'

(e) wèé húsè nịnị, ụ vâ dọ́ nịnị
    you-if ask (pl) you will get (pl)
    'if you (pl) ask, you (pl) will get'

(f) èé húsè, ẹ vâ dọ́
    they-if ask they will get
    'if they ask, they will get'

Set B

(a) màá hị̀ ịsá, mị̀ vâ rị́ ọ́
    I-if buy food I will eat it
    'if I buy food, I will eat it'

(b) wàá hị̀ ịsá, ụ vâ rị́ ọ́
    you-if buy food you will eat it
    'if you buy food, you will eat it'

(c) òọ́ hị̀ ịsá, ọ vâ rị́ ọ́
    he-if buy food he will eat it
    'if he buys food, he will eat it'

(d) yàá hị̀ ịsá, ị vâ rị́ ọ́
    we-if buy food we will eat it
    'if we buy food, we will eat it'

Figure 4. Dependent Clauses—Harmony Set A

		1st Person Singular	2nd Person Singular	3rd Person Singular	1st Person Plural	2nd Person Plural	3rd Person Plural	Tone
IF	Present Continuous	mèéè	wèée	èee	yèéè	wèéè ... nįnį	èéyè	L H M (L H L)
	Simple Past	mè é	wèé	òó	yèé	wèé ... nįnį	èé	L H
	Past Perfective	mèé sí	wèé sí	òó sí	yèé sí	wèé si ... nįnį	èé sí	L H H
	Future	mèé vè	wèé vè	òó vè	yèé vè	wèé vè ... nįnį	èé vè	L H HF
WHEN	Present Continuous	ḿ mèè	ú mèè	ó mèè	í mèè	ú mèè ... nįnį	é mèè	H L L
	Simple Past	ḿ mè	ú mè	ó mè	í mè	ú mè ... nįnį	é mèè	H L

Figure 4. Dependent Clauses—Harmony Set B

		1st Person Singular	2nd Person Singular	3rd Person Singular	1st Person Plural	2nd Person Plural	3rd Person Plural	Tones
IF	Present Continuous	màáa	wàáa	àáa	yàáa	wàáa . . . nįnį	ẹ̀ẹ́yà	L H M (L H L)
	Simple Past	màá	wàá	ọ̀ọ́	yàá	wàá . . . nįnį	ẹ̀ẹ́	L H
	Past Perfective	màá sị́	wàá sị́	ọ̀ọ́ sị́	yàá sị́	wàá sị . . . nįnį	ẹ̀ẹ́ sị́	L H H
	Future	màá vâ	wàá vâ	ọ̀ọ́ vâ	yàá vâ	wàá vâ . . . nįnį	ẹ̀ẹ́ vâ	L H HF
WHEN	Present Continuous	ḿ màà	ú màà	ô màà	í màà	ú màà . . . nįnį	é màà	H L L
	Simple Past	ḿ mẹ̀	ú mẹ̀	ô mẹ̀	í mẹ̀	ú mẹ̀ . . . nįnį	ẹ́ mẹ̀	H L

(e) wàá hị ịsá nịnị, ụ vâ rị ọ́ nịnị
   you-if buy food (pl)   you will eat it (pl)
   'If you (pl) buy food, you (pl) will eat it'

(f) èẹ́   hị ịsá, ẹ vâ rị ộ
   they-if buy food they will eat it
   'If they buy food, they will eat it'

Dependent clause WHEN

The preverb for WHEN dependent clause in the past simple tense in the VP is order 1 double preverb: ḿ mè (1s) for harmony set A verbs and ḿ mẹ̀ (1s) for harmony set B verbs.

Set A

(a) ḿ mè ré é, ộ   dàhí
   I- when see him he-is well
   'When I saw him, he was all right.'

(b) ú mè ré é, ộ   dàhí
   you-when see him he-is well
   'When you saw him, he was all right.'

(c) ó mè ré é, ộ   dàhí
   he-when see him he-is all right
   'When he saw him, he was all right.'

(d) í mè ré é, ộ   dàhí
   we-when see him he-is well
   'When we saw him, he was all right.'

(e) ú mè ré é nịnị, ộ   dàhí
   you-when see him (pl)   he-is well
   'When you (pl) saw him, he was all right.'

(f) é mè ré é, ộ   dàhí
   they-when see him he-is well
   'When they saw him, he was all right.'

The Verbal Piece: Phrase Rank

Set B

(a) ḿ mẹ̀ vẹ́,   mâ rḯ ịsá
    I-when come I   eat food
    'When I came, I ate food.'

(b) ú mẹ̀   vẹ́, wâ rḯ ịsá
    you-when come you eat food
    'When you came, you ate food.'

(c) ó mẹ̀ vẹ́,   ô rḯ ịsá
    he-when come he eat food
    'When he came, he ate food.'

(d) í mẹ̀   vẹ́, yâ rḯ ịsá
    we-when come we eat food
    'When we came, we ate food.'

(e) ú mẹ̀   vẹ́ nịnị, wâ rḯ ịsà nịnị
    you-when come (pl) you eat food (pl)
    'When you (pl) came, you (pl) ate food.'

(f) ẹ́ mẹ̀ vẹ́,   ê rḯ ịsá
    they-when come they eat food
    'When they came, they ate food.'

Note that only the WHEN dependent clause relationship is exemplified in the preceding section. WHEN as a question word and as a time-reference word has other forms in Ebira. Those forms are not discussed here as they are not signalled by preverbs within the VP.

4.8 Pluralization

Pluralization is normally a grammatical category within the nominal phrase in the structure of the clause. But in Ebira, where some clauses may not have an NP but only VP, pluralization is manifested in the preverb of the VP, except in one case: 2nd person plural. In 2nd person plural, the preverb is the same as 2nd person singular, and a plural marker, nịnị, is always appended to the VP. I will briefly describe pluralization in the NP and then expand more on the use of nịnị to pluralize elements in the VP.

Pluralization in the nominal phrase

The initial vowel singular/plural class system mentioned in §2.3 as a remnant from distant Bantu connection is limited to a few nominals and is not typical of Ebira pluralization. These are repeated here:

SINGULAR		PLURAL	
ọ̀zà	'a person'	àzà	'people'
ọnẹ́ẹ́	'a woman'	anẹ́ẹ́	'women'
onọrú	'a man'	anọrú	'men'
ọ̀zoga	'a visitor'	àzoga	'visitors
ọ̀hị́nị́	'a co-wife'	ẹ̀hị́nị́	'co-wives'
ozí	'child'	ezí	'children'
òsé	'wife'	èsé	'wives'

More commonly the language distinguishes between singular and plural in three ways, namely:

(a) by multiple nominal phrase,
(b) by using numerals,
(c) by using the plural marker particle *nịnị*.

Pluralization by listing a number of nouns. One way of indicating plural in Ebira is just by listing names of individuals as items in the NP of the clause.

```
okè, ịcà, ìzé, ocu ệ   vẹ́
Oke Ica Ize Ocu they came
        NP              VP
```
'Oke, Ica, Ize, Ocu, came.'

In this form of pluralization the preverb of the VP is always the plural form of the 3rd person, *e* or *ẹ*, except in the present continuous tense, where the singular form of the preverb is often used in the VP following a multiple NP as subject.

As already mentioned in §4.3, VP must include a preverb indicating person and number even if there is also a preceding NP subject.

```
okè  ộ  wụ  wá
Oke he kill them
```
'Oke killed them.'

The Verbal Piece: Phrase Rank

  okè o̱ni̱ri̱ ìzé è̱ vẹ́
  Oke and Ize they came
  'Oke and Ize came.'

In the next sentence following in the discourse, *okè* is likely to be pronominalized, and taken up by the resumptive pronoun *o/o̱* (according to harmony with the verb) and this pronoun is also the preverb. Similarly with *okè o̱ni̱ri̱ ìzé*, being taken up with *e/e̱*.

For pronoun subjects and objects see §5.9, Tables 1–3.

Pluralization by numerals. One other way of indicating plural in the language is by the use of specific numerals to qualify any noun in the NP.

(a) ezí è̱e̱va è̱ vẹ́
   children two they came
   N + NUM
   NP$_S$ VP
   'Two children came.'

(b) Okè ó̱ wu̱ uye è̱e̱nà
   Oke he kill animal four
   NP$_S$ VP NP$_O$
   'Oke killed four animals.'

Pluralization by particle marker, *ni̱ni̱*. The third and most common way of indicating pluralization is by the use of the plural particle marker, *ni̱ni̱*.

In the NP, *ni̱ni̱* can pluralize either noun or pronoun (whatever function the NP may have). It pluralizes nouns or pronouns which refer to animate beings, whether persons or animals.

ni̱ni̱ can also pluralize elements in the VP (although it is not itself an element of the VP) as follows:

1. a 2nd person pronominal preverb (subject);
2. a 2nd person pronominal object postverb.

These will be discussed and illustrated further in the next section. In all cases, tones on *ni̱ni̱* are as follows:

(a) mid-mid, *ni̱ni̱*, if it qualifies a pronoun, either a free pronoun or pronoun element in the VP;

(b) low-mid, *ni̱ni̱*, if it qualifies a noun.

The following examples will clarify the use of the two forms of nìnì/nini

(a) *nìnì,* qualifying nominal NPs and NPo
òzókú nìnì ê wu uye nìnì.
elder (pl) they kill animal (pl)
NPs   VP   NPo
'The elders killed the animals.'

(b) *nini,* qualifying a free pronoun and *nìnì* qualifying NPo
èwu nini é rê ezí nìnì.
you (pl) they see the children
PN NP   VP   NPo
'You (pl) saw the children.'

(c) *nini,* qualifying an element in the VP
wâ wu nini
you kill (pl)
    VP
'You (pl) killed.'

(d) *nìnì* qualifying the NPo of the VP and *nini* qualifying the pronominal subject element of the VP.
wâ wu uye nìnì nini.
you kill animal (pl) (pl)

    VP   NPo
'You (pl) killed the animals.'

(e) *nini,* qualifying object postverbs
okè ô ré wu nini
Oke he see you (pl)
NP   VP
'Oke saw you (pl).'

It can be observed from the above, particularly example (d), that the language employs low-mid tone for *nìnì* which pluralizes nominals and mid-mid tone for *nini* which pluralizes pronominals and both avoid semantic ambiguity.

The Verbal Piece: Phrase Rank

The use of *nịnị* to qualify elements in the VP

In all the Figures where preverbs signal various categories of the VP, the form for 2nd person singular and plural is the same. *nịnị* is appended to the VP to distinguish the plural from the singular. As already mentioned in the previous section, *nịnị* may qualify elements of the VP which refer to 2nd person plural, where the reference is to animate beings. Multiple NP and numerals are pluralization forms used for inanimate things.

Some representative examples of various categories of the VP where *nịnị* occurs to pluralize the 2nd person are given below.

The indicative positive: simple past

(a) wê hú   nịnị
    you drink (pl)
    VP   (pl)
    'You (pl) drank.'

(b) wê hú ọ́ nịnị
    you drink it (pl)
    VP   (pl)
    'You (pl) drank it.'

(c) wê hú ècè nịnị
    you drink wine (pl)
    VP   NP$_O$ (pl)
    'You (pl) drank wine.'

The interrogative mood: past perfective

wéé sì   ècè hú   nịnị
you have wine drink (pl)
VP   NP$_O$ (pl)
'Have you drunk wine?'

The imperative mood. Although the imperative mood has zero preverb, to distinguish a command to singular 2nd person and plural 2nd person, *nịnị* is just appended to the VP.

(a) nâ nịnị
    go (pl)
    VP (pl)
    'you (pl) go'

(b) hí ezí   nìnì nìnì
    call children (pl) (pl)
    VP NP₀   (pl) (pl)
    'You (pl) call the children.'

It is significant to note that *nìnì* is an independent plural marker of fixed form. It is not considered to be an element of the VP for two reasons:

1. All elements of the VP are governed by the harmony set of the verb, but *nìnì* is fixed in its form.
2. It may be separated from the VP by other elements of the clause, as illustrated in the simple past examples (b) and (c) above.

nìnì and *nìnì* are two fixed particles which have important syntactic and grammatical functions in the NP and VP of the language.

5 The Verbal Piece: Clause Rank

5.1 The Clause

As already described briefly in §4.2, the clause can be diagrammed as:

Cl → ± NP$_S$ + VP ± NP$_O$

The verbal phrase is the obligatory nuclear element of every verbal clause. Thus a clause may consist of just the verbal phrase. As already mentioned in chapter 4, the presence of NP$_S$ and NP$_O$ is determined by the nature of the verb and other grammatical options. This will be discussed further below. Expansion of the clause may occur either at the beginning of or at the end of the clause, such as locative phrase (LP), temporal phrase (TP), and adverbial phrase (AP). These are outside the scope of this description.

The function of the verb classes in the clause will be described in this chapter with particular reference to transitivity. The verb is the point of origin for the preverbs harmonically and the central point of reference for distinguishing various types of verbal clauses.

The following types of verbal clauses are distinguished in Ebira:

Transitive	§5.2
Distransitive	§5.3
Semitransitive	§5.4
Intransitive	§5.5
Stative	§5.6
Equative	§5.7
Copula	§5.8

Thus seven types of clauses are established according to the functions of the verb which is head of the clause and the nominal phrase elements of the clause which complement the verb in the transitivity system. These types will not be described in detail.

After the discussion of clause types, further features of the clause rank will be described, namely:

Pronoun System   §5.9
Interrogation and Interrogative Words   §5.10

5.2 Transitive Clause

The transitive clause is marked by a class of verbs which take direct NP objects. The majority of Ebira verbs belong to this class. Transitive clauses may occur in any mood, tense, polarity, person, or number. All transitive verbs express actions.

The structure of a transitive clause can be diagrammed as:

Trans Cl → ± NP$_S$ + VP + NP$_O$

NP$_O$ is an obligatory element which complements the verb in the transitive clause. Some common verbs used in transitive clauses include:

ré	'to see'	rị́	'to eat'
hú	'to drink'	dọ́	'to get'
hí	'to weave'	ná	'to sell'
cé	'to break'	hụ́	'to boil'

cèrè	'to write'
càká	'to break'

Some of these verbs will be used in the examples below to illustrate transivity in various categories.

(a) *izé ô   ré   ozí*
    Ize she see child
    (NP$_S$) VP   NP$_O$
    'Ize saw the child.' (indicative)

(b) *izé ọ̀nị̀rì àrí ê   ré   ozí*
    Ize and   Ari they see child
    - - - - - - - -
       (NP$_S$)   VP   NP$_O$
    'Ize and Ari saw the child.' (indicative)

Note that while it is possible to have sentences without an NP$_S$, the shape of the order 1 preverb shows the person and number of NP$_S$ which usually will have occurred previously in the discourse.

(c) ô ré ozí
    he see child'
    VP   NP$_O$
    'He saw the child.' (indicative)

(d) ê ré ozí
    they see child
    VP   NP$_O$
    'They saw the child.' (indicative)

(e) ẹ́ẹ́   ná enu
    they (inter) sell yams
    'Did they sell yams?' (interrogative)

(f) cẹ̀rẹ̀ ìwe
    write book
    'Write a book.' (imperative)

(g) ẹ̀   hì ìtà
    they (should) buy cloth
    'They should buy a piece of cloth.' (subjunctive)

5.3 Ditransitive Clause

Some ideas, which in many languages are expressed by ditransitive verbs, are expressed in Ebira by serial verb constructions (see chapter 6). There are, however, a few verbs which can occur in ditransitive clauses in the language. Ditransitivity has the feature of duality, i.e., two NP$_O$ are involved, the first being the recipient of the action. Like transitive clauses, ditransitive clauses may occur in any mood, tense, polarity, person, or number. The structure of ditransitive clauses can be diagrammed as:

Ditrans Cl → ± NP$_S$ + VP + NP$_{O1}$ + NP$_{O2}$

There are as yet just six verbs found in this class. They are:

zù 'to show someone something'
kọ́ 'to teach someone something'
kụ́ 'to shave (hair) for someone, to lift someone's legs'
jị 'to bite (someone) a bite'

dà 'to cut part of someone off'
círe 'to plant fear in someone'

The use of these verbs will be illustrated in the examples below.

(a) ộ zụ̀   ozí eva
    he show child oracle
       VP   NPo1 NP2
    'He showed the child the oracle.' (indicative positive)

(b) ọ́ yí kọ́ ọ̀zà iwe
    he not teach person book
        VP   NPo1 NPo2
    'He did not teach a person to read a book.' (indicative negative)

(c) mị̀ vâ kụ́ ọ̀mụ̀yà ịresụ́
    I will shave Omuya head
            VP   NPo1   NPo2
    'I will shave/trim Omuya's hair.' (indicative general future)

(d) irezí ọ́ọ́ jị̀ Izé ịrẹrú
    dog   it   bite Ize bite
    (NPs) VP   NPo1 NPo2
    'Did the dog bite Ize?' (interrogative past)

(e) ẹ̀ dà oyi uvọ́
    they cut thief hand
        VP   NPo1 NPo2
    'Let them cut off the thief's hand.' (subjunctive)

(f) ekú   ô cire ozí àŋwà
    masquerade he plant child fear
    (NPs)   VP   NPo1 NPo2
    'The masquerade frightened the child.' (indicative past)

Note the difference between relationships of the two NPo in a ditransitive clause as distinct from relationships in a genitive complex NP functioning as object:

1. Tone
2. Word Order

The Verbal Piece: Clause Rank

DITRANSITIVE CLAUSE

mâ kụ́   Ọ̀mụ̀yà ịrẹsụ́
I   shave/trim Omuya head
VP NP_{o1} NP_{o2}
'I shaved (to) Omuya's hair.'

GENITIVE NP_O

ộ ná ẹnụ   ọ́mụ̀yà
he sell yams (of) Omuya
VP NP_O
'He sold Omuya's yams.'

In the ditransitive clause, both NP_O have a direct relationship to the verb, the first being the recipient of the action.

In the genitive construction, however, the second NP element of the genitive complex NP is related directly to the first NP element, the first being the possessed item and the second the possessor. At the clause level, the complex NP functions as a unit.

In Ebira the genitive construction is used only to express possession. Many concepts which in English might be expressed by a genitive construction are expressed in Ebira by a ditransitive clause.

5.4 Semitransitive Clause

Semitransitive clauses are characterized by the occurrence of a verb expressing motion and a NP_O which semantically refers to a goal. The NP occurring as object always refers to a place. The NP_O cannot be pronominalized. This is an important feature of this type of clause. When the goal referred to is a person or a thing, the serial verb construction is used as in example (iii) below. For a detailed description of serial verb constructions (SVC), see chapter 6.

The structure of the semitransitive clause can be diagrammed as:

Semitrans Cl → ± NP_S + VP + NP_O ± TP

Some verbs which occur in semitransitive clauses include:

nọ   'to go'
vẹ́   'to come'
zwè   'to run'
hìrà 'to fly'
tùrà 'to crawl'

There are three ways of expressing the action 'to go' in Ebira:

(i) *nâ* 'always occurs in intransitive clauses':
    ộ   nâ
    he go
    VP
    'he went' (indicative past)

(ii) *nọ* 'always occurs in semitransitive clause which takes NP$_O$ as object':
    ô   nọ   eehí
    he go home
    VP   NP$_O$
    'he went home'

(iii) *na* occurs in complex verb constructions as an auxiliary verb. It cannot occur as clause final and it cannot take an object. It can only cooccur with another verb where 'motion to' is required (for further discussion see §6.4).
    ộ   na hị   ịtà
    he go buy cloth
    VP   NP$_O$
    'He went to buy cloth.'

(a) ozi èè tùrà àbàrà
    child he crawl room
    (NP)   VP   NP$_O$
    'The child is crawling in the room.' (indicative)

(b) vẹ́ áárẹ̣ ùhwọ́ọ́
    come farm tomorrow
    VP   NP$_O$ (TP)
    'Come to the farm tomorrow.' (imperative)

Note that *vẹ́*, 'come' can be used either semitransitively or intransitively, that is, in a semitransitive clause, or intransitive clause.

    ẹ́ẹ́ vẹ́
    they come
          VP
    'Did they come?' (interrogative past)

See the next section for further examples of intransitive clauses.

The Verbal Piece: Clause Rank 113

5.5 Intransitive Clause

The intransitive clause does not take an object. It has the following structure:

Intr Cl → ± NPs + VP

The intransitive clause can occur in any mood, tense, polarity, person, or number. Some common verbs used in the intransitive clause include:

nâ 'to go'
vẹ 'to come'
tá 'to be finished'
hẹ̀ 'to be retarded in growth'
hí 'to be full'
sú 'to die'
gụ 'to be complete'

(a) *ộ tá*
    it finish
        VP
    'It is finished.'

(b) *ozí ọnọ́ọ́ ộ hẹ̀*
    child that he (is) retarded
    NPs   VP
    'That child is retarded (in growth).' i.e.,
    'The child is a dwarf.' (indicative simple past)

(c) *ụnọ́kọ́ ô sí hí*
    pot it has full
    NPs   VP
    'The pot has been filled.' (past perfective indicative)

(d) *àdá Izí èè vê sú*
    father Ize he about die
    NPs   VP
    'Ize's father is about to die.' (immediate future indicative)

5.6 Stative Clause

The stative clause never has an object. The clause describes the state of something. The stative clause differs from the intransitive clause of the preceding section as follows:

(a) the stative clause can occur only in the indicative and interrogative moods, simple past, and future tenses. It cannot occur in the imperative and subjunctive moods, or in the habitual tense, whereas the intransitive clause can occur in all the grammatical categories.

(b) the verbs which occur in stative clauses are characterized by the fact that nouns can be readily derived from the verb roots by adding the nominalizer prefixes o-/-ǫ or u/u̧-:

báṇí	'to be big'	ǫ́báṇí	
		ubaṇí	'bigness'
wèyí	'to be small'	ówéyí	
		úwéyí	'smallness'
jóji	'to be black'	ójóji	'blackness'
kátá	'to be strong'	u̧kátá	'strength'
bu̧ru̧	'to be thick'	ǫbu̧ru̧	'thickness'

Prefixes cannot be added to the verbs that occur in the intransitive clause to derive nouns from them.

The structure of the stative clause can be diagrammed as:

Stat Cl → ± NP + VP

Some verbs which occur in stative clauses are listed below. It is interesting to note that they are all disyllabic in phonological structure.

báṇí	'to be big'
diví	'to be bad'
vòrò	'to be straight'
hérę́	'to be light'
rátá	'to be heavy'
gana	'to be wide'
ŋurá	'to be hot'
kátá	'to be strong'
wèyí	'to be small'
zózà	'to be good/beautiful'
ràrà	'to be twisted'
godǫ	'to be long/tall'
bu̧ru̧	'to be thick'
jóji	'to be black/dark'
hínê	'to be sweet'

Examples of these verbs in stative clauses are given below:

(a) ozí   Izé ọ̀ bánị
    child Ize he big
    (NPs)   VP
    'Ize's child is big.' (indicative simple past)

(b) oze ọ́ yị́ gana
    road it not wide
    (NPs)   VP
    'The road is not wide.' (negative polarity simple past)

(c) ẹná ọ́ọ́ rátá
    load it   heavy
    (NPs)   VP
    'Is the load heavy?' (simple past interrogative)

(d) ozí ọnọnị ọ́ yị́ vâ godo
    child this   he not will tall
    (NPs)   VP
    'This child will not be tall.' (future negative indicative)

5.7 Equative Clause

The equative clause expresses a descriptive relationship between two nominals. It exists in the indicative and interrogative moods and simple past and future tenses. It does not occur in the imperative and subjunctive moods nor in habitual, and present continuous tense categories. The structure of the equative clause can be diagrammed as:

Eq Cl → NP + VP + NP

So far only one verb has been found to occur in this clause. It is *vị* 'to be'. One may ask, is /vị/ a verb at all?

It is a verb and it constitutes a class of its own. Like other verbs it takes preverbs which harmonize with it, and like a majority of other verbs it has a CV structure.

(a) arí ọ̀ vị ọ̀kụ́rụkụ́
    Ari he be farmer
    NP(sg)   VP NP
    'Ari is a farmer.' (indicative mood)

(b) okè ọnịrị àrí ẹ̀   vị òsòhù nịnị
    [Oke and Ari] they be trader (pl)
    NP(pl)   VP   NP
    'Oke and Ari are traders.' (indicative)

(c) ẹ́nịnị ẹ́   yị́ vị ozube nịnị
    they they not be hunter (pl)
    NP   VP   NP
    'They are not hunters.' (negative indicative)

(d) àdá   izé ọ́ọ́ vị ògùeyí
    father Ize he be close eye person
    NP   VP   NP
    'Is Ize's father a blind man?' i.e.,
    'Is Ize's father blind?' (interrogative mood)

Note that *vị* can take only preverbs of set B because it belongs to that harmonic set.

5.8 Copula Clause

The copula clause expresses an identification relationship. It occurs only in the indicative mood and the interrogative mood of the prosodic type (see §5.10 for interrogation by a prosody).

The structure can be diagrammed as:

Cop Cl → NP + copula

Ebira has just two copulas which are *yọ́* 'it is' and *yị́* 'this is':

(a) idù   yọ́
    lion   it is
    NP   copula
    'It is a lion.' (indicative mood)

(b) oyí yọ́ ọ
    thief he is inter
    NP   copula
    'Is he a thief?' (interrogative mood)

(c) ikù   yị́
    scorpion this is
    NP   copula
    'This is a scorpion.' (indicative mood)

The Verbal Piece: Clause Rank

(d) ozí   àdíve   yị̂   ị
    child Adive this is inter
            NP   copula
    'Is this Adive's child?' (interrogative mood)

There is a distinction in the usage of the copulas yọ́ and yị́. yị́ is used for description, e.g., 'This is my father's house.' yọ́ asks or answers an identificational question.

sé vị ọnọ́ọ	'What is that?'
ènẹ́ vị ọnọ́ọ	'Who is that?'
irehi ámi yọ́	'It's my house'
àdá ámi yọ́	'He's my father'

5.9 The Pronoun System in the Clause

Pronominal pieces occur as nominal phrases functioning in the clause as NPs. They may also occur in subject relationship in the VP, as well as in object relationships in the VP, preverbs or postverbs respectively. When functioning in the VP, they are phonologically bound to other elements of the VP. As these pronominal pieces have different forms and functions in these positions within the clause, the full system is displayed in tabular forms below and examples given.

Table 1 shows the independent pronouns NP which may function as head of NPs in the clause.

Table 2 shows the pronominal pieces, part of VP but not NP, which (in combination with various tones) signal:

(a) tense as well as person and number;
(b) subject relationship of the VP in the clause.

Table 3 shows pronominal pieces, elements of the VP, which function as objects in the clause.

Table 1.   Independent Pronouns (NPs)

PERSON	NUMBER			
	SINGULAR		PLURAL	
1ST	èmị	I	èyi	we
2ND	èwụ	you	èwụ nịnị	you
3RD	onị	he, she, it	ẹ́ nịnị or ẹ́nị	they

The independent pronouns as NPs are normally used for emphasis, and in discourse for resumptive pronoun NPs.

ẹ̀mị̂ mâ rị́ ịsá
I   I   eat food
NPs   VP   NPo
'I ate the food.'

ẹ̀wụ wâ rị́ ịsá
you you eat food
NPs VP   NPo
'You ate the food.'

ọnị̀ ô rị́ ịsá
he   he eat food
NPs   VP NPo
'He ate the food.'

ẹ̀yị yê hú ècè
we   we drink wine
NPs VP   NPo
'We drank some wine.'

ẹ̀wụ wê hú ècè nịnị
you you drink wine (pl)
NPs VP   NPo   (pl)
'You (pl) drank some wine.'

énịnị ê hú ece
they they drink wine
NPs   VP   NPo
'They drank some wine.'

The pronoun subjects in the gloss translation in the above examples are usually emphasized by extra stress in English.

It can be observed in Table 1 and in the examples that all the independent pronouns belong to harmony set B. The preverbs following them in the clause agree with them in number and person but not in harmony. This confirms the validity of the pronouns as independent NPs.

It is of interest that all independent grammatical words have vowels of set B. These include the independent pronoun subjects above, the negative imperative word ásụ́ in §4.6, the plural marker nịnị in §4.8, the copulas yọ́ and yị́ in §5.8, and the preposition ị́nị́ in §6.4.

The Verbal Piece: Clause Rank

Table 2. Pronominal piece (preverb), element of the VP, may function as subject.

PERSON	NUMBER			
	SINGULAR		PLURAL	
1ST	mi, me/mị, mẹ, ma	I	i, ye/ị, yẹ, ya	we
2ND	u, we/ụ, wẹ, wa	you	u, we/ụ, wẹ, wa ... nịnị	you
3RD	o/ọ	he, she, it	e/ẹ	they

See Charts 1–4 in chapter 4 for detailed description of the preverbs.

Table 3. Pronominal piece (postverb), elements of the VP, functions as object.

PERSON	NUMBER			
	SINGULAR		PLURAL	
1ST	mi/mị	me	yi/yị	us
2ND	wu/wụ	you	wu/wụ nịnị	you
3RD	-ó, -ə́[1]	him, her, it	wá	them

The following examples illustrate the pronominal postverb pieces as part of VP in the clause.

1ST PERSON SINGULAR - SET A

    izé   ô   sì   mi
    Ize   she look for me
    NPs   VP
    'Ize looked for me.'

---

[1] ə represents nonclose vowels.

1ST PERSON SINGULAR – SET B

    ìzé ộ hị́ mị̀
    Ize she call me
    NP_S   VP
    'Ize called me.'

2ND PERSON SINGULAR – SET A

    okè ô tú wu
    Oke he beat you
    NP_S   VP
    'Oke beat you.'

2ND PERSON SINGULAR – SET B

    okè ộ tụ̀ wụ
    Oke he pull you
    NP_S   VP
    'Oke pulled you out.'

3RD PERSON SINGULAR – SET A

    ìze ô hị́ ọ̀
    Ize she weave it
    NP_S   VP
    'Ize wove it.'

3RD PERSON SINGULAR – SET B

    ìze ộ hị́ ọ́
    Ize she call him
    NP_S   VP
    'Ize called him.'

3RD PERSON SINGULAR – SET A

    ịcà ô hú ọ́
    Ica he drink it
    NP_S   VP
    'Ica drank it.'

The Verbal Piece: Clause Rank

3RD PERSON SINGULAR – SET B

    ịcà ộ hụ̀ ọ́
    Ica he open it
    NP_S   VP
    'Ica opened it.'

The following additional examples are given without person, set A and B, NP_S, and VP labels.

    Ocu ô ne é
    Ocu he throw it
    'Ocu threw it.'

    Ocu ộ mẹ̀ ẹ́
    Ocu he do it
    'Ocu did it.'

    Ocu ô nò ó
    Ocu he knead it
    'Ocu kneaded it.'

    Ocu ộ họ ọ́
    Ocu he fence it
    'Ocu fenced it.'

    Ocu ộ ná á
    Ocu he sell it
    'Ocu sold it.'

The following examples illustrate plural pronominal postverb pieces.

    ẹnịnị ê tú yi
    they they beat us
    'They beat us.'

    ẹnịnị ệ dụ yị
    they they chase us
    'They chased us.'

    ekú ô tú wu nịnị
    masquerade he beat you (pl)
    'The masquerade beat you (pl).'

ekú   ọ̀   du   wu   nịnị
masquerade he chase you (pl)
'The masquerade chased you (pl).'

ekú   ô   tú   wá
masquerade he beat them
'The masquerade beat them.'

ekú   ọ̀   du   wá
masquerade he chase them
'The masquerade chased them.'

It can be observed from Table 3 and the examples that the 3rd person singular has interesting forms harmonically and phonologically.

For 3rd person singular:

(a) -ọ́: occurs as pronominal object when the final vowel of the verb is one of the close vowels, *I* and *U*;

(b) -ǎ: when the final vowel of the verb is a nonclose vowel, *E, O, A*, this vowel is lengthened for pronominal object.

For 3rd person plural there is just one form, *wá*, for pronominal object for both harmony sets A and B.

For the pronouns, high tone is a shared feature for singular and plural forms of the pronominal object 3rd person pieces, and mid tone for 1st and 2nd person singular and plural pieces.

5.10 Interrogation and Interrogative Words in the Clause

Most clause types described so far can occur in the interrogative mood which is evinced by a particular verbal phrase with specific preverbs (§4.5). There are two other ways of transforming indicative clauses into questions. These are:

(a) by a prosodic system of the language
(b) by the use of question words

Interrogation by prosodic element

Any indicative clause can be transformed into a question by simply reduplicating the final vowel of the item in clause-final position, the added vowel carrying mid tone and constituting a syllable on its own.

The added final vowel is a prosodic element of the entire clause and a feature of the interrogative mood.

The Verbal Piece: Clause Rank

This type of interrogative mood always requires a YES or NO answer. These are referred to as polar questions.

The structure of the clause can be diagrammed thus:

Cl → ± NP + VP ± NP$_O$ + $ə^2$

As elsewhere, mid tone is not marked.

(a) *Izé ô ré ozí i*
    Ize she see child inter
    (NP$_S$) VP NP$_O$
    'Did Ize see the child?' (transitive clause, polar question)

(b) *ọ́ vẹ́ ẹ*
    he come inter
        VP
    'Did he come?' (intransitive polar question)

(c) *Okè ọ́ kụ́ ozí ịrẹsụ́ ụ*
    Oke he shave child head inter
    (NP$_S$) VP NP$_{O1}$ NP$_{O2}$
    'Did Oke shave the child's hair?' (ditransitive polar question)

(d) *Icà vị oyí i*
    Ica is thief inter
    NP VP NP
    'Is Ica a thief?' (equative clause, polar question)

Interrogative words

There are some particles in the language which are used to introduce particular content questions of the clause. They are similar to 'wh' question words of English.

ịsị́	'what'
izị́	'where'
ịhị́	'when (specific day, time, reference)'
ènẹ́	'who'
sẹ́vẹ́ dị́	'why'
meme/mẹmẹ	'how'

---

[2] *ə* is a prosodic element representing any vowel phoneme of the language.

(a) ịsị ọ́ mẹ̀
 what he do
       VP
 'What did he do?'

(b) ịzị ụ́ yá
 where you be
       VP
 'Where are you?'

(c) ịhị ọ́ vẹ́
 when he come
       VP
 'When (which specific day) did he come?'

(d) ẹnẹ̣ ó ré
 who he see
       VP
 'Who did he see?'

(e) sẹvẹ dị́ ụ́ càká á
 why   you break it
              VP
 'Why did you break it?'

(f) ụ́ mẹ̀mẹ̀ mẹ̀ ẹ́
 you how   do it
         VP
 'How did you do it?'

With one exception, *mẹmẹ/meme* 'how', interrogative words occur before the VP in the clause, irrespective of their grammatical relationship to the verb.

The exception *mẹmẹ/meme,* 'how', occurs within the VP, after the pronominal preverb, and preceding any other preverbs and the verb. It is of interest that, because it occurs within the VP, its vowel sequence is governed, with respect to harmony, by the vowels of the verb.

(a) ụ́ mẹ̀mẹ̀ cẹ̀rẹ̀ ẹ́
 you how   write it
 quest   VP
 'How did you write it?'

(b) ú mèmè pèhé é
   you how winnow it
   quest   VP
   'How did you winnow it?'

An alternative analysis would be to consider *mẹmẹ/meme* as a preverb being part of the VP. However, interrogative words substitute for phrase units which are elements of the clause, e.g., for NP₀, NPs; *mẹmẹ/meme* substitutes for an adverbial phrase (how, this is how). Therefore it is considered as a feature of the clause, like other interrogative words.

Question: ọ́ mẹ̀mẹ̀ àà vẹ́
   he how is come
   prvb quest VP
   'How is he coming?'

Answer: umátò àà sí vẹ́ nị̀³
   (by) car he-is take come narr
   AdvP   VP
   'He is coming by car.'

---

³*nị* is a particle that has a syntactic function in discourse, in that it always ends a declarative or a narrative statement.

   ẹkura ọbanị ọ́ vị̀ nị
   city   big   it is narr
   'It is a big city.'

See the narrative story in chapter 7 for further examples of *nị*.

6 The Verbal Piece: Serial Verb Constructions

6.1 The Serial Verb Construction

The serial verb construction, SVC for short, is a syntactic phenomenon found in many languages of West Africa, especially the Kwa group of the Niger-Congo family. It is an important aspect of the verbal system of Kwa languages which has attracted the attention of many linguists for some time. The phenomenon has been called by various names such as "string verbs," "verbal combinations," "verbs in series" and "compressed sentence constructions." Modern scholars, including some indigenous West African linguists like A. Bamgbose (1972, 1974, 1982), O. Awobuluyi (1967, 1973), and I. George (1975), who have written extensively on this verbal structure, seem to have reached a consensus in adopting the term "serial verb construction." I use that label in this chapter in which the structure as it exists in Ebira is briefly described. Occasional references are made to Yoruba or Nupe to point out similarities and differences since these languages are related to one another.

6.2 Syntactic Characteristics of Serial Verb Constructions in Kwa Languages

The syntactic characteristics of SVC are featured in a clause or a sentence by a sequence of two or more verbs or verb phrases without any overt connective word between them.

These series of verbs in the clause share a single subject and often a single object. They also share the same preverbs. The following examples from Ebira, Yoruba and Nupe will illustrate the occurrence of these verbs in the sentence.

Ebira:

> oké ọ̀ vẹ vá sị́ àpáànà
> Oke he come come take gun
> 'Oke came and took a gun.'

Yoruba:

> olú wá gbé ibọn
> Olu come take gun
> 'Olu came and took the gun.'

Nupe:

> tsoda bé lá egbà
> Tsoda come took axe
> 'Tsoda came and took the axe.'

It can be observed from the above examples that the notion expressed by a series of two or three verbs in the three languages can be expressed in English by two verbs and a connective or by two verbs and a preposition. Sometimes the notion expressed by two serial verbs in serial verb languages may be expressed by one verb in English.

The serial verb construction is a complex structure which can occur in grammatical categories of the VP described in Ebira in chapters 4 and 5. These will be exemplified in the remaining sections of this chapter. All the verbs functioning as part of a series in SCV will always share the same categorial features, i.e., they will share the same mood, tense, person and number, and polarity, and not have these categories indicated separately for the different verbs of the SCV.

6.3 The Verbal Status of Serial Verbs

There are several types of criteria by which verbal status may be determined in Ebira. The primary criterion is function in the verbal phrase. Secondary criteria are syllable structure and tonal pattern; all verbs have a distinctive phonological pattern. Judged by these criteria, each of the words in bold face type in the three sentences above is potentially an independent verb except *vá* which is the auxiliary form for *vé*, 'to come'. (The auxiliary verbs are described in §6.5. For syllable structure of verbs, see §2.1; for tone and tone patterns on verbs, see §2.6.)

It will be described further how verbs in series function as heads of verbal clauses and convey a composite notion as opposed to how each verb in the series functions independently and conveys its inherent lexical meaning. The following example is sufficiently illustrative at this point.

ìzé ọ̀ sị́ ècè vẹ́
Ize she take wine come
'Ize brought some wine.'

In the above sentence Ebira serial verbs sị́ and vẹ́ express an action which is expressed in English by one word, *bring* (with past tense, *brought*). The two Ebira verbs which express the concept of bringing have their individual meanings apart from the concept of bringing. They can be used independently of each other as follows:

(a) sị́   'to take'

ọ̀ sị́ ẹná ọ́báṇí
he take load big
'He took a big load.' i.e., 'He carried a big load.'

(b) vẹ́   'to come'

ọ̀ vẹ́ èèrị́
he come yesterday
'He came yesterday.'

In the serial verb construction, sị́ and vẹ́ combine to function as the head of the VP of the indicative clause.

Function is the main criterion by which we categorize individual verbs and serial verbs in sentence constructions.

6.4 Types of Serial Verb Constructions in Ebira

Four types of serial verb constructions are found in Ebira. These include:

1. Concomitant serial verb construction
2. Coordinate serial verb construction
3. Comparative serial verb construction
4. Complex serial verb construction

Each of these types is described in the context of category options in which they occur with illustrative examples.

Concomitant serial verb construction

In the concomitant serial verb construction, two or three verbs are jointly used to express a concept. It may be possible for such a concept to be expressed in another language by a single but semantically composite verb. The concomitant SVC can occur in indicative and interrogative moods; all the tenses; either polarity; 1st, 2nd or 3rd person; and singular or plural. But most of the examples are in the indicative.

An account of a limited number of common verbs in concomitant verb serialization surveyed is briefly given below.

Two action verbs which occur very frequently in serialization are:

sí̩   'to take, to carry'
yí̩   'to give'

Two motion verbs which also occur frequently in serialization are:

nâ/na   'to go'
vé̩/vá   'to come'

(Note that these are allomorphs, not harmony sets.)

Two location verbs which occur in serialization are:

tú̩   'to be on/in'
gé̩   'to hang on, to put on'

The verb sí̩ 'to take'. Although both sí̩ and yí̩ occur very frequently in concomitant serialization, the two verbs behave differently with regard to syntactic order.

sí̩ never occurs as the last verb in a series.
yí̩ always occurs last in a series.

sí̩ can be said to be the most common and the most complex of all the serial verbs of Ebira. It can cooccur with almost any other verb in serial combination. It can even cooccur with itself in some cases. Its semantic interpretation varies from context to context. In most cases it combines with the other verb or verbs in series to represent composite concepts.

Examine the following occurrences of sí̩ in various sentences.

(a) ocu ò̩ sí̩ ù̩hwò̩
    Ocu he take knife
    'Ocu took a knife.'

(b) *ocu ọ̀ sị́ ụ̀hwọ̀ vẹ́*
Ocu he take knife come
'Ocu brought a knife.'

(c) *ocu ọ̀ sị́ ụ̀hwọ̀ dà ẹnụ*
Ocu he take knife cut yam
'Ocu cut the yam with a knife.'

(d) *ocu ọ̀ sị́ ụ̀hwọ̀ yị́ ìzé*
Ocu he take knife give Ize
'Ocu gave the knife to Ize.'

(e) *ocu ọ̀ sị́ ụ̀yà rị́ ozí*
Ocu he take suffering eat child
'Ocu punished the child.' or 'Ocu caused the child to suffer.'

(f) *ocu ọ̀ sị́ ụvọ́ sị́ ọ́ yị́ mi*
Ocu he take hand take it give me
'Ocu gave it to me by hand.'

It is not intended here to go into an exhaustive semantic interpretation and analysis of each occurrence of *sị́* in the above serial combinations. However, a brief remark will illustrate the frequency and the complexity of *sị́* in serial combination with other verbs.

Sentence (a) is the only example above in which *sị́* carries its primary lexical meaning in the sentence. In sentences (b) to (f) the composite meaning conveyed by the verbs in series differs from one to the other, although *sị́* is shared by all. In sentences (e) to (f) the English verbs representing the composite meanings of the Ebira verbs in series have prepositions attached to them. One can observe that a concept conveyed by two different word classes in English, i.e., preposition and verb, is conveyed in Ebira by the verb alone. It is a general observation that Kwa languages very rarely make use of prepositions syntactically, but use verbs to express relationships such as instrument, direction, and accompaniment (and many others) which in other languages, English in particular, are expressed by prepositions.

As yet there is just one preposition, *íṇí,* found in Ebira. This preposition is used to cover the semantic areas normally conveyed by the English prepositions *into, inside, among.*

ocu ọ̀ yà íṇí eehí
Ocu he is inside house
'Ocu is inside the house.'

ocu ộ nọ ị́nị́   ibánki
Ocu he go inside bank
'Ocu went to the bank.'

ocu ộ yà ị́nị́ aza   ọnị   eku   tú
Ocu he is in people which masquerade beat
'Ocu is among the people the masquerade beat.'

okè ọnịrị ocu ệ   ŋu   ị́nị́ eehí
Oke and Ocu they enter inside house
'Oke and Ocu went into the house.'

Note that *ị́nị́* is another grammatical word which does not harmonize with any other form; it is invariable. (See the note in §5.9 for a comment on independent grammatical words.)

The verb *yị́* 'to give'. As mentioned in the preceding section, *yị́* is another verb that occurs frequently in serial construction. It never occurs as VP1 in the series but it can occur as a single independent verb in a sentence. It can occur in a transitive clause as in this sentence:

ìzé ô   yị́ ozí   ịsá
Ize she give child food
'Ize fed the child.'

In serial construction *yị́* normally occurs in transitive clauses where there are direct and indirect objects. The first verb in the series, where there are only two verbs, may be labelled VP1 and the second verb may be labelled VP2. The VP1, which may be any transitive verb, is followed by the direct object, and *yị́*, which is always the VP2, is followed by the indirect object. But *yị́* is in serial relationship with VP1 as they both share one NP and the same preverbs.

(a) *ìzé ộ   sị́   ịsa yị́   ozí*
    Ize she take food give child
    'Ize gave food to the child.'

(b) *okè ộ hị̀ ịta yị́ òsé anị*
    Oke he buy cloth give wife his
    'Oke bought a piece of cloth for his wife.'

(c) *okè ô cé irecé yị́ òhínọ́yị́*
    Oke he lie lie give chief
    'Oke lied to the chief.'

(d) okè ọ̀ mẹ̀ ụkọ́rọ yị́ òhínọ́yị́
    Oke he do work give chief
    'Oke works for the chief.'

All four preceding Ebira sentences have the same structure. VP2 extends and complements the meaning of VP1. Together the two verbs give a composite meaning of the VP in the sentence.

Comparing *sị́* and *yị́*, we can observe that there is order of sequence in serial verb constructions. Some verbs can occur as VP1 and others can occur as VP2 only. With regard to these two commonest verbs in SVC, *sị́* always occurs as VP1 and *yị́* always occurs as VP2, as already indicated. We can notice further that the notion conveyed by one or other of the verbs in a SVC is usually carried by the preposition in English. A. Bamgbose (1982:7), commenting on this particular aspect, remarks:

> There is no reason why a notion expressed by one language through a preposition or an adverb cannot be expressed through a verb by another language. This is the whole basis of differentiating functions of the verb in an SVC.

Motion verbs *nâ* 'to go' and *vẹ́* 'to come' in serial verb constructions. The motion verbs *nâ* and *vẹ́* are another pair in serial verb constructions. The two verbs have variant forms that occur in specific clause types and syntactic order.

The motion verb 'to go' has three forms as mentioned earlier in §5.4:

nâ occurs in intransitive clauses
nọ occurs in semitransitive clauses
na occurs in serial verb constructions.

The motion verb 'to come' has two forms:

vẹ́ occurs in intransitive and semitransitive clauses
vá occurs in serial verb constructions.

Whenever *na* and *vá* occur in an SVC the notion of 'purpose' is introduced into the sentence. These two forms of 'to go' and 'to come' in SVC can be labelled auxiliary verbs. They do not occur as independent VPs, but always occur with other independent verbs. For this reason they can cooccur with their other independent forms in sentences. Examine the following:

(a) ọ́ nâ na rị́ ịsá
    he go go eat food
    'He went (in order to) eat food.'

(b) ọ́ vẹ́ vá hị̀ ịtà
   he come come buy cloth
   'He came (in order to) buy cloth.'

The above is one occasion where it is possible to have three verbs in series in a sentence, although one is auxiliary and always introduces the semantic notion of purpose. There are very few auxiliary verbs in the language. They are described in §6.5. Whenever the idea of purpose is introduced into an action where motion is involved an auxiliary verb is used as in:

(c) ô na dá ọcị̣́
   he go cut tree
   'He went and cut the tree.'

(d) ộ vá ná ẹnụ
   he came sell yam
   'He came and sold yams.'

By way of comparison with the neighboring Kwa language, Yoruba serial verb constructions differ from Ebira serial verb constructions with regard to the number of verbs in similar constructions. Yoruba uses two verbs where Ebira may use three. Yoruba has just one form for the motion 'to go', lọ, and the motion 'to come', wá. The following sentences illustrate the comparison:

Ebira: okè ộ nâ na rị́ ịsá
       Oke he go go eat food
       'Oke went and ate food.'

Yoruba: olú lọ jẹ onjẹ
        Olu go eat food
        'Olu went to eat food.'

It may be pointed out also that Yoruba does not have the preverbs in the verb pieces as does Ebira. Ebira serial verb constructions are more complex in some respects than Yoruba serial verb constructions.

Locative verbs *tụ́* and *gẹ́* in serial verb constructions. Two verbs which occur in concomitant serial verb constructions in Ebira are:

tụ́ 'to put on, to put under'
gẹ́ 'to hang on'

These verbs always occur as VP$_2$ in serialization with particular reference to a location. They can only occur with sị́, 'to take', as VP$_1$.

(a) okè ọ̀ sị́ ẹná tụ́ ịrẹsụ́ ága
    Oke he take load put head chair
    'Oke put the load on the chair.'

(b) okè ọ̀ sị́ ẹná tụ́ ịrùvò ága
    Oke he take load put bottom chair
    'Oke put the load under the chair.'

(c) okè ọ̀ sị́ àmù gẹ́ ọcị́
    Oke he take cap hang tree
    'Oke hung the cap on the tree.'

In sentence (a) *sị́ - - -tụ́* in relation to *ịrẹsụ́* 'head' gives the concept 'put on.' Similarly, in (b) *sị́ - - -tụ́* in relation to *ìrùvò,* 'bottom,' gives the concept 'put under.' In sentence (c) *sị́ - - -gẹ́* gives the concept of 'hang on'.

Note that body nouns are used to express specific parts of a location normally expressed by prepositions in English. In (c), where there can be no semantic ambiguity, the body names are not used.

Note that *sị́* occurs in all three sentences but its basic meaning is not obvious at all in the composite meaning of the verbs. This illustrates a case in which the total meaning of the verbs in series form one concept and become more important than the individual meaning of each verb. This is typical of concomitant verb serialization.

Coordinate serial verb construction

In the coordinate SVC, two verbs are used in a sentence in a particular sequential order. The action expressed by VP1 precedes that of the VP2. Where there is a sequence of transitive verbs which share the same NP$_0$ semantically, that NP$_0$ is expressed overtly only in the first NP of the series. Each verb in a coordinate SVC always carries the meaning it would have in a simple sentence.

(a) okè ọ̀ hị̀ uye rị́
    Oke he buy meat eat
    'Oke bought meat and ate it.'

(b) ìzé ọ̀ vwọ̀ ụ̀kà vẹ́
    Ize she cook uka come
    'Ize cooked uka and brought it.'

In a coordinate SVC, it is possible to have two transitive verbs in one sentence as in (a) above. It is also possible to have a transitive verb and an intransitive verb as in (b) above.

One characteristic of the coordinate SVC sentence is that it can be extended to have two parts joined by a coordinate connective, *dí,* and then have a terminal particle marker, *nị* added. The introduction of the coordinate connective and a terminal particle alters the style of the sentence. Note this:

(c) okè ọ̀ hị̀ uye d'ọ́   rị́ ọ́ nị
    Oke he buy meat and–he eat it narr
    'Oke bought meat and ate it.'

In English, sentences (a) and (c) have the same translation but in Ebira there is a stylistic difference. Sentence (a) is used in conversation and in descriptive discourse while sentence (c) is used in narrative discourse. Serial verb construction is not just a surface syntactic phenomenon, it is a stylistic and a semantic feature of the language.

The following verbs are frequently used together in coordinate SVC:

VP1		VP2	
hị̀	'to buy'	rị́	'to eat'
mè	'to make'	ná	'to sell'
kà	'to move'	vé̩	'to come'
pà	'to beg'	rị́	'to eat'
và	'to turn'	nâ	'to go'

It is of interest to note the tonal features of these verbs. All the verbs in VP1 are monosyllabic low tone verbs, and all the verbs in VP2 are monosyllabic high or high-falling tone verbs. This is an unexpected feature but it has been observed to be true in all the examples which have been examined. This tonal regularity may not necessarily be the case when disyllabic or multisyllabic verbs are involved.

Comparative serial verb construction

Comparatives involving size, length, width, and weight are normally expressed in SVC structures in Ebira. Stative verbs and one specific comparative verb, *hu* 'more/less' or 'more than/less than', characterize this structure. The following sentences illustrate the degrees of comparison in the language.

(a) ákù izé ọ̀ bánị́
    room Ize it–is big
    'Ize's room is big.'

(b) àbàrà okè ọ̀ banị́ hu àkù izé nị
    room Oke it–is big more room Ize narr
    'Oke's room is bigger than Ize's.'

(c) àbàrà àrì ọ̀   baṇí hu   kere-kere nị
    room Ari it–is big more ideophone narr
    'Ari's room is the biggest.'

The verb *hu* 'to be more than or less than' is the only comparative verb that occurs in the comparative SVC in Ebira. To get the notion of superlative degree, an ideophone, *kere-kere*, is always appended to the VP *hu*, resulting in a composite meaning of 'more than, than' or 'less than, than'.

Some verbs used in comparative SVC include:

wèyí	hu	'smaller than'
gana	hu	'wider than'
gọdọ	hu	'longer/taller than'
hẹ́rẹ́	hu	'lighter than'

Complex serial verb construction

Complex serial verb constructions involve some abstract concepts normally expressed by one verb in English. Complex SVC results from the fact that neither of the two verbs in series has direct connection with the composite meaning of the verbs put together. Furthermore, the complex SVC has a fixed collocation of verbs. Both verbs must be present for the sentence to be meaningful.

(a) ocu ọ̀ dọ́ okè wụ́
    Ocu he get Oke hear
    'Ocu believed Oke.'

(b) okè ọ̀ dọ́ izé há
    Oke he get Ize save
    'Oke saved Ize.'

Common verbs in complex SVC are:

dọ́ - - wụ́	'to believe'
dọ́ - - há	'to save'

The difference between the concomitant serial verb construction and the complex serial verb construction is that, in the complex type, the meaning of the two verbs taken together is one concept, which cannot be derived from the meaning of the two parts taken separately. In the concomitant type, however, the composite meaning can be derived from the meaning of the verbs which make up the series. In the coordinate type, each verb retains its separate meaning unmodified.

6.5 Auxiliary Verbs

Auxiliary verbs differ from other verbs in that auxiliary verbs cannot occur independently functioning as heads of verbal phrases. In respect of phonological structure, however, auxiliary verbs have the same structure as other verbs. They always retain their harmony set. There are only three auxiliary verbs found in Ebira as yet. For two of them, *na* and *vá*, there are apparently related forms which can occur independently in the clause. (See §5.5)

The three auxiliary verbs are:

zụ́ 'can'
na 'to go'
vá 'to come'

na and *vá* are already described in §6.4.

Examples are given here for *zụ́* only.

   ọ̀ zụ́ rị́ ịsá
   he can eat food
   'He can eat food.'

   ô zụ́ zwè ècí
   he can run run
   'He can run.'

The description of the serial verb construction in Ebira is by no means exhaustive in this chapter. My aim has been to highlight the most important aspects of the SVC in relation to the total verbal system of the language.

7 Analyzed Text

An Ebira folk tale is presented in this chapter, together with a representation of an analysis of various units of the verbal piece. The fable is a typical narrative normally told to the child during the evening moonlight entertainment in a compound home. I heard the story when I was young and I recently recorded, edited, and transcribed it. There are many fables about the hare and the tortoise in the language. This is just one of them. In this fable, the hare is said to be older than the tortoise.

The narrative is presented as follows:

- Line a: gives a broad phonetic transcription, showing vowel elisions and tone changes of connected speech;
- Line b: gives a phonemic word-by-word transcription with all the tones;
- Line c: gives a literal word-for-word translation;
- Line d: gives phrase level analysis;
- Line e: gives clause-level analysis;
- Line f: gives a free idiomatic translation;
- Line g: gives a grammatical category label.

A single bar (/) indicates phrase breaks, a double bar (//) marks the end of dependent clauses, and a triple bar (///) indicates the end of a sentence.

SVC indicates serial verb construction in the phrase or in the sentence.

The following abbreviations are used for types of clauses in line four:

dep trans cl	dependent transitive clause
ind trans cl	independent transitive clause
dep semitrans cl	dependent semitransitive clause
in semitrans cl	independent semitransitive clause
dep intr cl	dependent intransitive clause
ind intr cl	independent intransitive clause
eq cl	independent equative clause
ind cop cl	independent copula clause
dep stat cl	dependent stative clause

The Text

The Hare and the Tortoise

1. a) *uhyádéjì* *oniròpàkú* *yí*
   b) *uhí* *àdéjì* *oniri* *òpàkú* / *yí* ///
   c) fable hare and tortoise this is
   d)   NP   VP
   e) ind cop cl
   f) This is a fable of the hare and the tortoise.
   g) Indicative mood.

2. a) *ekúhyònâ* *àdéjóhyópàkú*
   b) *ekúhí* *ònâ* / *àdéjì* / *ò* *hí* *òpàkú* ///
   c) day one hare he call tortoise
   d)   P (intro)   NP   VP
   e) ind trans cl
   f) One day the hare called the tortoise.
   g) Indicative mood.

3. a) *d' ókàárịhịnị* //
   b) *dí* *ò* *ka* *àárịhịnị*
   c) and he say please
   d)   VP
   e) dep intr cl
   f) And he said please

   a) *ò* *vá* *sàasóni* *nidótáni* *ni*
   b) *ò* *vá* *sàasá oni no ídá òtá áni ni* /// SVC
   c) he come follow him go place friend his narr
   d)   VP
   e) ind semitrans cl
   f) He should please go with him to his friend's house.
   g) Subjunctive mood.

4. a) *d' òpàkú* *kooho* *ni*
   b) *dí* *òpàkú* / *ka* *ooho* *ni* ///
   c) and tortoise say O.K. narr
   d)   NP   VP
   e) ind semitrans cl
   f) And the tortoise said, "All right".
   g) Indicative mood.

Analyzed Text

5.
a) ijékúhị̂   sị́ tù   d' énìnàà   nâ nị
b) ịjị́ ekụ́hị̂ sị́ tù //   dị́ énìnị àà nâ nị ///
c) when day has reach   and they are going narr
d)   NP   VP   NP   VP
e) dep intr cl   indep intr cl
f) They started going when the day came.
g) Indicative mood.

6.
a) àdéjóhyopàkwózè   d' ọ́ka   yèé túzọ́ọ
b) àdéjì / ộ hị́ ọ̀pàkụ́ òzè // dị́ ộ ka // yèé tù   ízọ́ọ //
c) hare he call tortoise road and he say if-we reach there
d)   NP   VP   VP   VP
e)   dep trans cl   dep intr cl   dep semitrans cl
f) Half way, the hare called the tortoise and said, "When we get there,

a) ọ̀tám   ọ̀ọ́ sísa   vẹ́
b) ọ̀tá ámị / ọ̀ọ́ sị́ ísa vẹ́   // svc
c) friend my   if-he take food come
d)   NP   VP
e)   dep trans cl
f) If my friend brought food,

a) navọ́ ma vìdị rísa   dúwa vâ   rísa   o
b) navọ́ ma vìdị́ rị́ ịsa // dị́ wa vâ rị́ ịsa o ///
c) wait I first eat food   and you will eat food mood
d)   VP   VP
e)   dep trans cl   ind trans cl
f) Let me eat first before you eat."
g) Subjunctive mood.

7.
a) d' ọ́pàkụ́ kẹ̀nẹ́   vọnụ́rà
b) dị́ ọ̀pàkụ́ ka // ẹ̀nẹ́ vị   ọnụ́rà ///
c) and tortoise say who be fool
d)   NP   VP   NP VP NP
e)   dep intr cl   ind eq cl
f) The tortoise asked, "Who is a fool?"
g) Interrogative mood.

8. a) *oӡówéyó   vòrò kò   vìdí rísá*
    b) *ozí ówéyí / ò   vòrò ka // ò vìdí rí isá //*
    c) child small   it-is right that   he first eat food
    d) NP   VP   VP
    e)   dep stat cl   dep trans cl
    f) The younger person ought to eat first

    a) *d' ózókwò   vá rísa   ni*
    b) *dí òzókú   ò vá rí isá ni ///*
    c) and older person he will eat food narr
    d) NP   VP
    e) ind trans cl
    f) before the older person should eat.
    g) Subjunctive mood.

9. a) *ìjénìnì   túzóọ*
    b) *ìjí ènìnì tù   ízóọ //*
    c) when they   reach there
    d) NP   VP
    e)   dep semitrans cl
    f) When they got there,

    a) *d' ádéjì wèrè   na kàá yótání   ka*
    b) *dí àdéjì / wèrè na kà á yí òtá ání ka //* SVC
    c) and hare quietly go tell it give friend his that
    d) NP   VP
    e)   dep tr cl
    f) the hare secretly went to tell his friend that

    a) *ìjòó   sísá   vé*
    b) *ìjí òó   sí isá vé //* SVC
    c) when if-he take food come
    d)   VP
    e)   dep trans cl
    f) when he brings food,

    a) *ò   kàá   yópàkú   ka*
    b) *ò   kà á   yí òpàkú ka //* SVC
    c) he-should tell it give tortoise that
    d)   VP
    e)   dep trans cl
    f) he should tell the tortoise

Analyzed Text

a) ọ̀ sàásọ́nị na denị óswe àgùví ka
b) ó sàásá ọnị na dà enị óswe àgùví ka // SVC
c) he-should follow him go fetch water at-spring because that
d)   VP
e)   dep trans cl
f) to go with him to the spring (place) because

a) enọ́ tá o
b) enị ộ tá o ///
c) water it finish mood
d) NP VP
e) ind intr cl
f) the (drinking) water is finished.
g) Indicative mood.

10. a) d' ọ́tá déjì kooho nị
   b) dí ọ̀tá àdéjì / ka ooho nị ///
   c) and friend hare say O.K. narr
   d)   NP   VP
   e)   ind trans cl
   f) The hare's friend agreed.
   g) Indicative mood.

11. a) ịjọ́sị́sa vẹ́
   b) ịjị́ ộ sị́ ịsá vẹ́ // SVC
   c) when he take food come
   d)   VP
   e) dep trans cl
   f) When he brought some food,

a) d' ọ́kọ̀pàkwọ̀ sáasọ́nị nóswe nị
b) dí ộ ka / ọpàkụ́ / ọ̀ sàasá ọnị no óswe nị /// SVC
c) and he say tortoise he-should follow him go spring narr
d)   VP   NP   VP
e)   ind semitrans cl
f) he told the tortoise to follow him to the spring.
g) Subjunctive mood.

12. a) ịjé sí hu dádéjì rísọ́nọ́ọ sáásáká
   b) ịjị́ é sí hu / dí àdéjì / rị́ ịsá ọnọ́ọ sáká-sáká //
   c) when they have gone and hare eat food that completely
   d)   VP   NP   VP
   e)   dep trans cl
   f) When they left the hare ate all the food

144 The Verbal Piece in Ebira

a) *d' ó sí zwe na tẹ nị*
b) *dí ó sí zwe na tẹ̀ nị ///*
c) and he has run go hide narr
d)   VP
e)   ind intr cl
f) and he ran away to hide.
g) Indicative mood.

13. a) *ịjọ́pàkụ́ ọnirọ̀tádéjì vẹ́*
  b) *ịjị́ ọ̀pàkụ ọnirị ọ̀tá àdéjì / vẹ́ //*
  c) when tortoise and friend hare come
  d)   NP   VP
  e) dep intr cl
  f) When the tortoise and the hare's friend came,

a) *ê ʃàdéjì póóró ê yí ré é*
b) *ê sì àdéjì póóró // ê yí ré é ///*
c) they look for hare long time they not see him
d)   VP   VP
e) dep trans cl   ind trans cl
f) they looked for the hare everywhere. They could not find him.
g) Indicative mood.

14. a) *uŋwàá kwọ̀pàkụ́ ètèètẹ̀rẹ̀*
  b) *uŋwẹ / àà kù ọ̀pàkụ́ ètẹ̀rẹ̀-ètẹ̀ẹ̀rẹ̀ ///*
  c) hunger it-is bite tortoise very well
  d) NP   VP
  e) ind trans cl
  f) The tortoise was very hungry.
  g) Indicative mood.

15. a) *d' ọ́pàkụ́ ka pàá*
  b) *dí ọ̀pàkụ́ / ka pàá*
  c) and tortoise say never
  d) NP   VP
  e) dep trans cl
  f) The tortoise vowed never

Analyzed Text

    a)   *ọnọ́ma   vàna sàasádejì   jị́nẹ   nị*
    b)   *ọnị / ọ́ ma   vàna sàasá àdéjì jị̣nẹ   nị*   /// svc
    c)   he   he never again follow hare go out narr
    d)   NP   VP
    e)   ind trans cl
    f)   to go anywhere with the hare.
    g)   Indicative mood.

16. a)   *hụ́rı́hyọnọ́ọ   hụ́rı́hyọnọ́ọ*
    b)   *hụ́rẹ́ ị̀hì ọnòọ hụ́rẹ́ ị̀hì ọnọ́ọ*
    c)   from day that from day that
    d)   AdvP   AdvP
    e)   general concluding phrase
    f)   From that day

    a)   *ọ̀pàkwọ́nịràdéjì   ẹ́   ma   zịzị   nị*
    b)   *ọ̀pàkụ́ ọnịrị àdéjì / ẹ́   ma   zịzị   nị* ///
    c)   tortoise and hare   they never go about narr
    d)   NP   VP
    e)   ind intr cl
    f)   the tortoise and the hare never went out together.
    g)   Indicative mood.

17. a)   *ọ̀họ̀hoyı́   zẽ   kàdéjọ̀nọ́tóbóóró*
    b)   *ọ̀họ̀há / óyị   zẽ   ka // àdéjì / ọ̀   ɲı́ ọ̀tá ọ̀bóóro* ///
    c)   greediness it-not allow that hare   he-should have friend proper
    d)   NP   VP   NP   VP
    e)   dep intr cl   ind trans cl
    f)   The hare never had a true friend because of greediness.
    g)   Indicative mood.

Appendix A

A Chart Of Monosyllabic Verbs

		i	į	e	ẹ	a	ọ	o	ụ	u
p	H					x				
	M					x		x		
	L					x	x			
	HF									
	LR									
b	H				x			x		
	M					x				
	L			x		x				
	HF									
	LR									
t	H				x	x	x		x	x
	M									
	L				x		x	x	x	x
	HF	x								
	LR									
d	H					x	x			
	M					x			x	x
	L					x				x
	HF									
	LR									
k	H					x	x		x	x
	M					x				
	L					x			x	x
	HF									x
	LR									
g	H				x				x	x
	M					x			x	
	L					x			x	x
	HF									
	LR									

		i	ị	e	ẹ	a	ọ	o	ụ	u
v	H	x	x		x	x	x		x	x
	M		x			x	x			
	L					x	x		x	
	HF									
	LR									
s	H	x	x		x	x			x	x
	M			x	x	x				
	L	x			x				x	
	HF									
	LR									
z	H	x		x		x	x		x	
	M		x							
	L	x		x					x	
	HF									x
	LR				x					
h	H	x	x	x		x			x	x
	M	x				x	x		x	x
	L	x	x		x	x	x		x	x
	HF									
	LR				x					
c	H	x	x	x						
	M									
	L	x								
	HF									
	LR									
j	H					x				
	M	x	x							
	L	x								
	HF									
	LR					x				

Appendix A

		i	į	e	ę	a	ọ	o	ụ	u
m	H	x				x				
	M					x	x			
	L				x					
	HF									
	LR									
n	H			x		x				
	M		x	x		x	x			x
	L			x		x		x		
	HF					x				
	LR						x			
ɲ	H	x	x			x				
	M		x							
	L	x								
	HF									
	LR				x					
ŋ	H									
	M				x				x	
	L					x				
	HF									
	LR									
r	H		x	x	x	x				
	M						x			
	L						x	x		
	HF									
	LR			x				x		
w	H				x	x		x	x	x
	M								x	x
	L					x				x
	HF									
	LR									
y	H	x	x	x	x	x	x			
	M									
	L					x				
	HF	x								
	LR									

Appendix B

A List Of Monosyllabic Verbs

The following is a list of monosyllabic verbs with their meaning.

pá	'to train or raise up a child'
pa	'to play tricks'
pà	'to beg'
pọ̀	'to be cheap'
po	'to mix flour in liquid'
bè	'to ambush, to trap someone'
bẹ́	'to carve (wood)'
ba	'to fast'
bà	'to dig'
bó	'to be old'
tî	'to sigh, to groan'
tẹ́	'to be made ashamed'
tẹ̀	'to hide'
dá	'to light a fire'
da	'to display wares'
dà	'to cut'
dụ	'to chase'
du	'to be spoiled'
dù	'to clear bush for farming'
ká	'to get water or grains with a cup from a big container'
ka	'to say'
kà	'to fish in a small river by damming and clearing the water away'
kọ́	'to teach, to learn'
kụ́	'to gather'
kụ̀	'to play football'
kú	'to foam or water to boil over'
kù	'to be late'
ku	'to happen in ancient times'
gẹ́	'to sew'
ga	'to praise in song'
gà	'to share'
gụ́	'to take side with'
gụ	'to be complete'
gụ̀	'to plant yam seedling'
gú	'to thatch a house'

gù	'to close (a door)'
ví	'to be ripe'
vi̧	'to be ready (cooked food)'
vi̧	'to be, is'
vȩ́	'to come'
vá	'to marry'
va	'to break dry wood'
và	'to pour'
vó̧	'to be left, part of something'
vo̧	'to cut meat in large pieces'
vʷò̧	'to make flour meal'
vú̧	'to put on trousers/pants or skirt'
vù̧	'to be rotten'
vú	'to be lost'
sí	'to pay'
sì	'to look for, to want'
sí̧	'to take'
sʷe	'to initiate something'
sȩ́	'to chop off grass'
sȩ	'to come true (predictions or prophecy)'
sȩ̀	'to bargain, to market'
sʷá	'to be smooth'
sa	'to be bland, to lose taste'
sú	'to die'
zí	'to lie in wait for someone'
zì	'to sieve'
zi̧	'to wander'
zé	'to be enough'
zʷè	'to run'
zě	'to agree to'
zá	'to catch'
zʷó̧	'to be scarce'
zú̧	'can, able'
zù	'to fall (rain)'
zu	'to tie up an animal to a tree'
hí	'to be full'
hi	'to string (beads)'
hì	'to sweep'
hí̧	'to call'
hì̧	'to buy'
hé	'to excrete body waste'
hě	'to be in possession of something by finding it'

Appendix B

hè	'to be retarded in growth'	
há	'to split wood with an axe'	
ha	'to wake up'	
hà	'to bark (a dog)'	
hǫ	'to drive, to pilot'	
hò	'to ask'	
hụ́	'to boil'	
hu̦	'to grow'	
hù̦	'to open'	
hú	'to drink'	
hu	'to uproot'	
hù	'to roast (in fire)'	
cí	'to get a load down off head'	
cì	'to press down in order to level'	
cí̦	'to germinate (seeds)'	
cé	'to break'	
ji	'to separate two people from fighting'	
jì	'to jump'	
ji̦	'to cut off a leaf or twig'	
jé̦	'to be happy'	
jě	'to wait'	
mí	'to put out light or fire'	
mè̦	'to do'	
má	'to fell (a tree)'	
ma	'to give birth'	
mǫ	'to measure (grains) with measuring cup'	
ni̦	'to be clean'	
né	'to trigger off (trap)'	
ne	'to throw'	
nè	'to prepare (gravy)'	
ná	'to sell'	
na	'to open'	
nà	'to tear'	
nâ	'to leave'	
nǫ	'to go'	
nǒ̦	'to make announcement with a special gong'	
nò	'to knead'	
nu	'to leak'	
ɲí	'to laugh'	
ɲì	'to cut a tooth'	
ɲí̦	'to have'	
ɲi̦	'to choose'	

ɲě	'to wipe'
ɲá	'to hit with hand'
ɲǎ	'to crack nuts with stones to get the seeds out'
ŋʷe̩	'to spin wool or cotton'
ŋʷà	'to loosen, to untie'
ŋu	'to enter'
rí̩	'to eat'
ré	'to see'
rě	'to lick the fingers'
ré̩	'to be sharp (knife)'
rá	'to inhabit (a place)'
ro̩	'to pour liquid through a funnel'
rò̩	'to be easy'
rò	'to think'
rǒ	'to make a hole through a wall'
wé̩	'to sharpen a hunting stick'
wá	'to carve a pointed stick'
wà	'to dig in the sand'
yí	'to steal'
yî	'to refuse'
yí̩	'to give, this is'
yé	'to understand'
yé̩	'to know'
yá	'to be bent'
yà	'to be in a place'
yó̩	'it is'

Appendix C

On the following pages are SAMPLE SPECTOGRAMS of my pronunciation showing words of contrastive vowel harmony sets.

156   Verbal Piece in Ebira

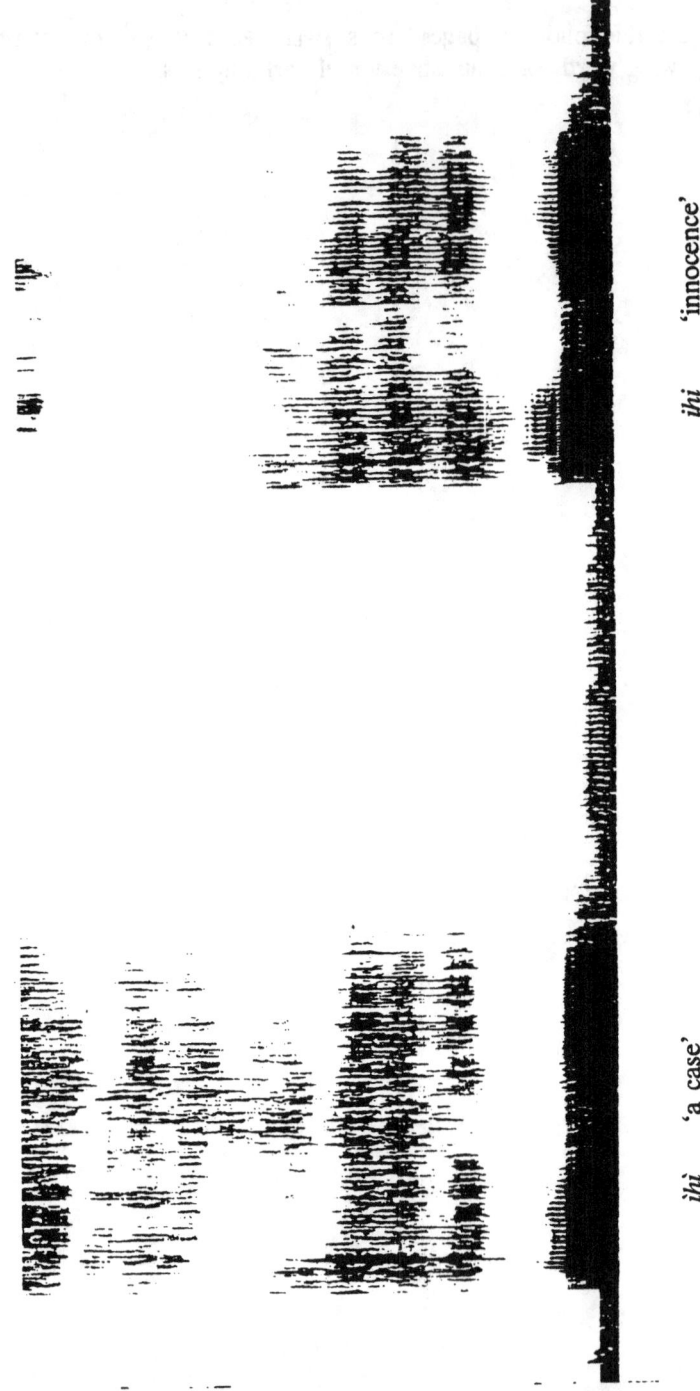

Appendix C

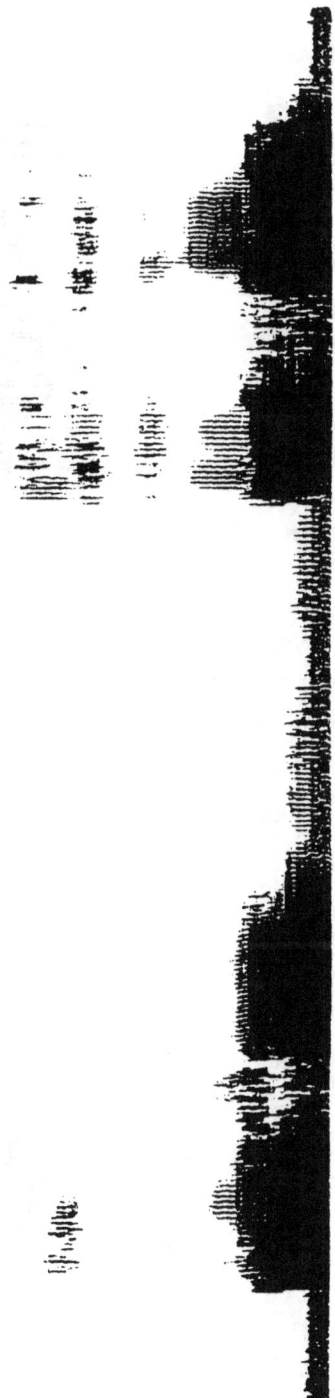

158   Verbal Piece in Ebira

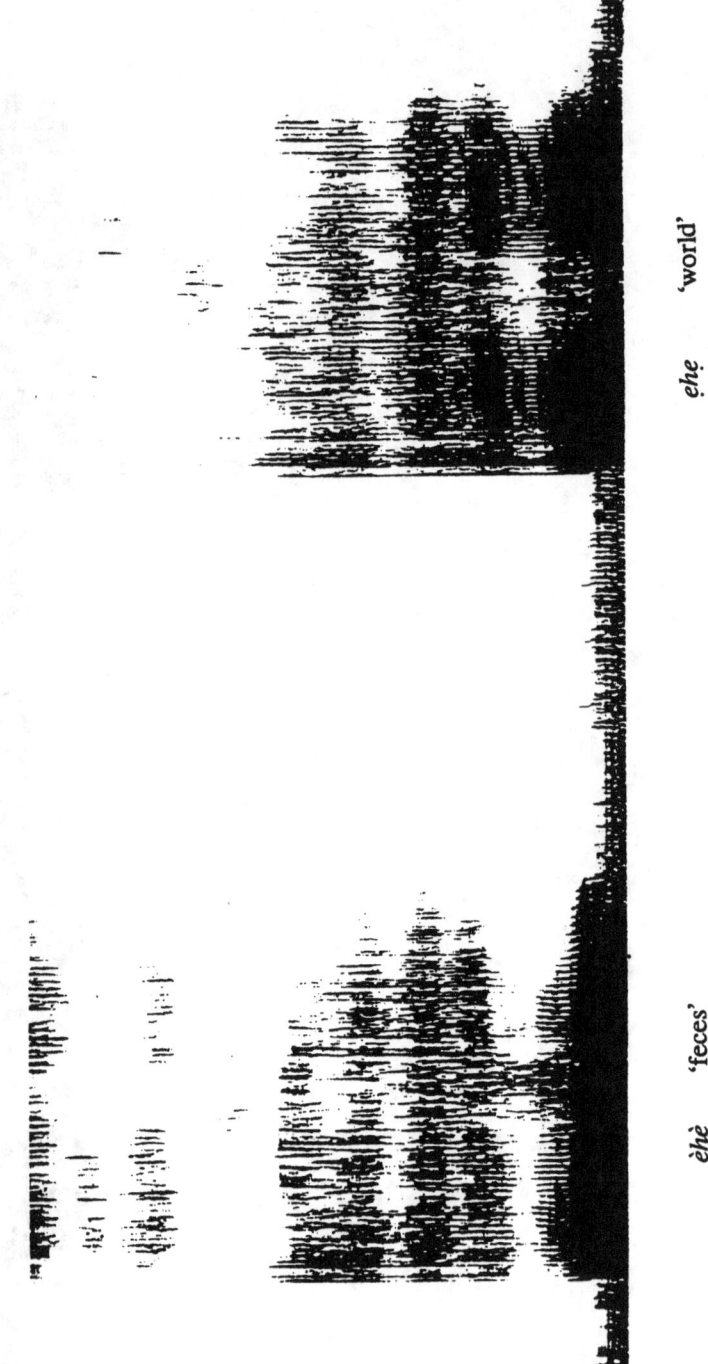

Appendix C

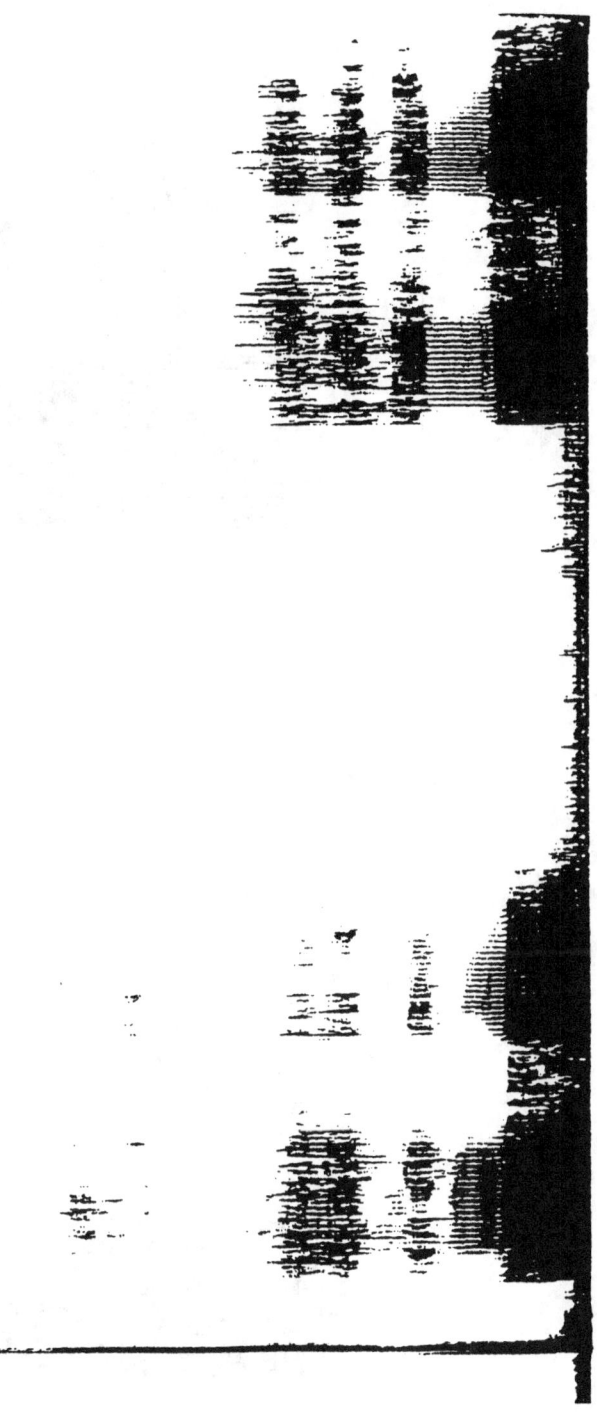

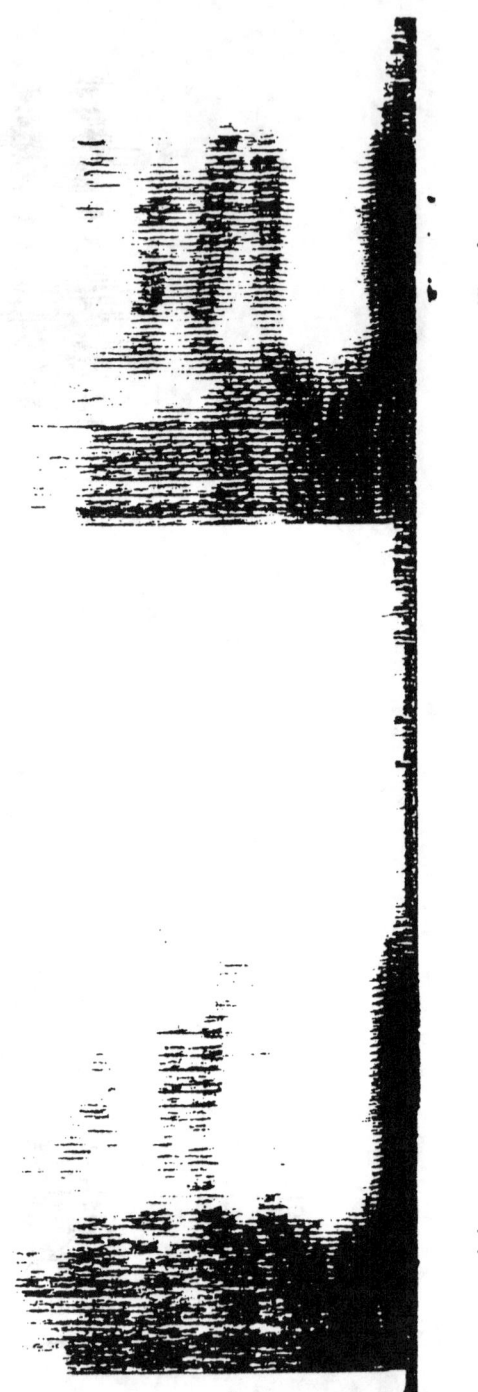

Bibliography

Awobuluyi, O. 1967a. Studies in the syntax of the standard Yoruba verb. Ph.D. dissertation, Columbia University.

———. 1967b. Vowel and consonant harmony in Yoruba. *Journal of African Languages* 6:1–8.

Bamgbose, Ayo. 1967. Vowel harmony in Yoruba. *Journal of African Languages* 6:268–73.

———. 1971. The verb-infinitive phrase in Yoruba. *Journal of West African Languages* 8.1:37–42.

———. 1982. Issues in the analysis of serial verbal constructions. *Journal of West African Languages* 12.2:3–21.

Barnwell, Katharine. 1969. A grammatical description of Mbembe. Ph.D. dissertation, London.

Bendor-Samuel, John T. 1960. Some problems of segmentation in the phonological analysis of Terena. *Word* 16:348–55. Republished in *Prosodic Analysis*, ed. by Frank R. Palmer. Oxford University Press (1970), pp. 214–21.

———. 1961. *The verbal piece in Jebero*. Word monograph 4 (Supplement to *Word* 17).

Bergman, Richard. 1971. Vowel Sandhi and word division in Igede. *Journal of West African Languages* 8.1:13–25.

Brown, Paula. 1955. The Igbira. In *People of the Niger-Benue confluence*, ed. by Daryll Forde. (Ethnographic Survey of Africa: Part X, West Africa) London: International African Institute, pp. 55–74.

Carnochan, Jack. 1960. Vowel harmony in Igbo. *African Language Studies* 1:155–63. Republished in *Prosodic analysis*, ed. by Frank R. Palmer. Oxford University Press (1970), pp. 222–29.

———. 1964. Pitch, tone, and intonation in Yoruba. In *In honour of Daniel Jones: papers contributed on the occasion of his eightieth birthday 12 September 1961*, ed. by David Abercrombie and others. London: Longmans, pp. 397–406.

———. 1970. Categories of the verbal piece in Bachama. In *African Language Studies XI*. London: School of Oriental and African Studies, pp. 81–112.

Chumbow, Beban Sammy. 1982. Contraction and tone polarization in Ogori. *Journal of West African Languages* 12.1:89–103.

Clarke, J. 1848. *Specimens of dialects*. Berwick-on-Tweed: Daniel Cameron.

Cust, R. N. 1883. *A sketch of the modern languages of Africa*, Vol. 1.

Dolphyne, Florence A. 1965. The phonetics and phonology of the verbal piece in the Asante dialect of Twi. Ph.D. dissertation, London.

Elimelech, Baruch. 1974. Tone alternation in the Etsako verb. *Working Papers in Phonetics* 27.

Elugbe, Ben Ohi. 1983. The vowels of Proto-Edoid. *Journal of West African Languages* 13.1:79–90.

Elemanjo, E. 'Nolue. 1982. The interfix: an aspect of universal morphology. *Journal of West African Languages* 12.1:77–88.

Faraclas, Nicholas. 1982. Elision and other morpheme boundary phenomena in the Western dialects of Obolo. *Journal of West African Languages* 12.2:69–82.

Firth, J. R. 1948. Sounds and prosodies. *Transactions of the Philological Society*. pp. 127–52. Republished in *Prosodic analysis*, ed. by Frank R. Palmer. London: Longmans, pp. 1–26.

Fromkin, Victoria A. 1972. Tone features and tone rules. *Studies in African Linguistics* 3:47–76.

George, Isaac. 1976. A grammar of Kwa type verb serialization: its nature and significance in current generative theory. Ph. D. dissertation, UCLA.

Greenberg, Joseph H. 1970. *The languages of Africa*. Bloomington: Indiana University.

Bibliography

Hansford, Keir, John Bendor-Samuel, and Ronald Stanford. 1976. *An index of Nigerian languages*. (Studies in Nigerian Languages, No. 5) Tamale: Summer Institute of Linguistics.

Hayward, R. J. 1976. Categories of the predicator in Afar, with special reference to the grammar of radical extension. Ph.D. dissertation, London.

Hoffman, C. 1976. The languages of Nigeria by language family. In *An index of Nigerian languages*, ed. by K. Hansford, J. T. Bendor-Samuel, and R. Stanford. (Studies in Nigerian Languages No. 5) Tamale: Ghana.

Hombert, Jean-Marie. 1977. Development of tones from vowel height? *Journal of Phonetics* 5:9–16.

Hyman, Larry M., ed. 1980. *Noun classes in the grassfields Bentu borderland*. (Southern California Occasional Papers in Linguistics, 8) Los Angeles: University of Southern California.

Hyman, Larry M. and Russel G. Schaub. 1974. Universals of tone rules: evidence from West Africa. *Linguistic Inquiry* 5:81–115.

Johnson, H. and J. Christaller. 1886. *Vocabularies of the Niger and the Gold Coast, West Africa*. London.

Koelle, S. W. 1854. *Polyglotta Africana*. London.

Ladefoged, Peter. 1964. Igbirra notes and word-list. *Journal of West African Languages* 1.1:27–37.

———. 1968. *A phonetic study of West African languages*. 2nd ed. Cambridge.

Lightner, Theodore M. 1965. On the description of vowel and consonant harmony. *Word* 21:244–50.

Marchese, Lynell. 1982. Basic aspectual categories in Proto-Kru. *Journal of West African Languages* 12.1:3–23.

Omamor, Augusta Phil. 1982. Tense and aspect in Isẹkiri. Journal of West African Languages 12.2:95–129.

Oyelaran, Ọlasope O. 1973. Yoruba vowel co-occurrence restrictions. *Studies in African Linguistics* 4:155–82.

Palmer, Frank R. 1965. *A linguistic study of the English verb*. London: Longmans.

———. 1976. *Semantics: a new outline*. Cambridge University Press.

Palmer, Frank R., ed. 1970. *Prosodic analysis*. London: Oxford University Press.

Picton, J. 1968. Concerning God and man in Igbirra. *Bulletin of the Institute of African Studies* 5.1:33–37.

Pike, Kenneth L. 1967. Tongue-root position in practical phonetics. *Phonetica* 17.3:129–40.

Robins, Robert H. 1957. Aspects of prosodic analysis. In *Prosodic Analysis*, ed. by F. R. Palmer. London: Oxford University Press (1970).

———. 1964. *General linguistics: an introductory survey*. London: Longmans. xxii, 390 pp.

Salami. A. 1972. Vowel and consonant harmony and vowel restriction in assimilated English loan words in Yoruba. In *African Language Studies* XIII. London: School of Oriental and African Studies, pp. 162–81.

Scholz, Hans-Juergen. 1976. *Igbirra phonology*. (Language Data Microfiche: African Series No. 7) Huntington Beach, California: Summer Institute of Linguistics.

Smith, N. V. 1961. A phonological and grammatical study of the verb in Nupe. Ph.D. dissertation, London.

Stewart, J. M. 1967. Tongue root position in Akan vowel harmony. *Phonetica* 16:185–204.

Thomas, N. W. 1914. *Specimens of languages from southern Nigeria*. London.

Ward, Ida C. 1952. *An introduction to the Yoruba language*. Cambridge.

Westermann, Dietrich and M. A. Bryan. 1952. *The languages of West Africa*. London: Oxford University Press.

Williamson, K. 1965. *A grammar of the Kolokuma dialect of Igo*. (West African Language Monograph Series No. 2) Cambridge University Press.

Wolf, Paul P. de. 1971. *The noun class system of Proto-Benue-Congo*. (Janua Linguarum, series practica 67) The Hague: Mouton.

www.ingramcontent.com/pod-product-compliance
Lightning Source LLC
Chambersburg PA
CBHW060955230426
43665CB00015B/2210